YOU CAN ACT!

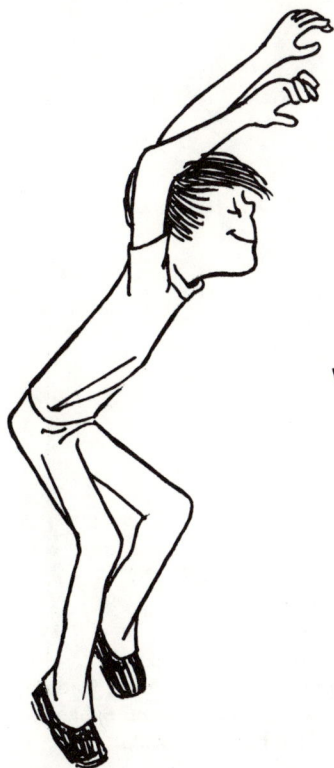

By Lewy Olfson

with drawings by SHIZU

S **STERLING**
PUBLISHING CO., INC. NEW YORK

Oak Tree Press Co., Ltd.
London & Sydney

OTHER BOOKS OF INTEREST

Masks

Best Singing Games for Children

Conditioning Your Memory

Humorous Monologues

Pantomimes, Charades and Skits

Puppet and Pantomime Plays

Puppet-Making

For Adele Thane

of the Boston Children's Theatre:

All roads lead to Oz

Third Printing, 1972

COPYRIGHT © 1970 BY PENDULUM PRESS, INC.

Copyright © 1971 by

Sterling Publishing Co., Inc.

419 Park Avenue South, New York, N.Y. 10016

Distributed in Canada by Saunders of Toronto, Ltd., Don Mills, Ontario

British edition published by Oak Tree Press Co., Ltd., Nassau, Bahamas

Distributed in Australia by Oak Tree Press Co., Ltd.,

P.O. Box 34, Brickfield Hill, Sydney 2000, N.S.W.

Distributed in the United Kingdom and elsewhere in the British Commonwealth

by Ward Lock Ltd., 116 Baker Street, London W 1

Manufactured in the United States of America

All rights reserved

Library of Congress Catalog Card No.: 76-151715

ISBN 0-8069-7016-2   UK 7061 2296-8

7017-0

CONTENTS

A Word to Young Actors

You can act. Yes, you can!

Have you ever played house, or cowboys and Indians? That's acting.

Have you ever read a story out loud? Or changed your voice to sound like different people in the story? That's acting.

Have you ever put on a circus in your back yard? Or a magic show? Or a play in your garage? That's acting.

Have you ever listened to music and just moved around to express the way the music made you feel? That is a kind of acting, too.

Acting is fun. And it's easy.

You can act with your body.

You can act with your voice.

You can even act when nobody can see you at all — if you have a puppet or a mask or a tape recorder or record player to help.

On the next page you will find a list of defined words that explain some of the things that go into acting. Remember it's there, and refer to it when you want.

When you've practiced a bit, you and your friends can put on real plays.

You can have all sorts of fun when you act. So turn to page 12 and begin right away.

Glossary

ACTING. Using words and moving your body in such a way as to tell a story.

ACTION. An action is the movement of the body in a certain way, such as running or climbing. The action of a play is the way in which things happen — one thing leading to another.

ACTOR. Any person who uses words and actions to tell a story.

AUDIENCE. The people who watch other people acting.

CHARACTER. A make-believe person in a play.

CHORAL READING. A kind of play where groups of actors all say the same thing at the same time.

CHORUS. A group of people who give a choral reading or singing.

DIALOGUE. The words used by people when they act.

EMPHASIS. The way in which people speak when they want the important words to stand out. They may say these words louder or slower, for example.

EXPRESSION. The way in which people use words, looks or actions to show different feelings.

FANFARE. The sound of trumpets or bugles or other noises to show that someone important is arriving, in a play.

GESTURE. A movement of the face, hands or shoulders, in such a way that it tells something. For example, you know that if you wave your hand one way it means "Good-bye." If you wave it another way it means "Come here."

MASK. Any covering for the face, or sometimes just the upper part of the face, used by people when they act.

MIME. To imitate somebody or something, as in a pantomime.

NARRATOR. The person who reads or tells about the action of a play, while the actors act it out.

PANTOMIME. Acting out a story without using words, but only gestures and movements.

PART. All the words and actions that belong to a certain character in a play.

PLAY. A story told by actors. Plays may be put on with real people as actors, or with imaginary people such as puppets as characters.

PUPPET. A hollow doll with an opening in its back. The doll becomes an imaginary actor when you put your hand inside and make it move.

READER. A reader, like a narrator, tells a story while other people act it out.

REHEARSAL. When the actors get together and practice all the dialogue and actions of a play, it is called a rehearsal.

REHEARSE. To practice the dialogue and actions of a play.

SCENES. The parts of a play are called scenes. When the actors are supposed to move to another place, or when the audience is supposed to imagine seeing them later in the day, or the next day — that is a change of scene.

SOUND EFFECTS. Noises made to imitate such sounds as thunder, falling rain, horses' hoofs, and other things.

A Word to Teachers

Say the word "dramatics," and most teachers think: "Let's put on a play."

To which I reply, "Let's *not* put on a play. Let's do lots of dramatics-oriented activities, but for Heaven's sake, let's *not* put on a play."

Not that there is anything inherently wrong with putting on plays. Indeed, there is a good deal that's right with such activity. But in most elementary schools, putting on a play is the sum total of work with dramatics, and it is this lopsided emphasis that must be corrected. As a culmination to certain kinds of classroom learning experiences, putting on a play is great. As a group activity that teaches the rewards of sustained effort and the pleasures of individuals working together toward a collective goal, it's fine. But as a one-and-only exposure to dramatics, putting on a play leaves a great deal to be desired.

Consider some of the things that dramatics activities can achieve that the particular activity of putting on a play cannot achieve:

■ Dramatics activities can involve every child in the class — as much or as little as he wishes.

■ Dramatics activities can make the participating child the chief creating force.

■ Dramatics activities can lead the child to an unselfconscious exploration and discovery of his own personality.

■ Dramatics activities can provide spontaneous excitement and motivation. The effort can be fun.

■ Dramatics activities can be self-contained events occupying less than five minutes of time.

- Dramatics activities can illuminate many areas of the curriculum.
- Dramatics activities can tap well-springs within a child that will then flow freely throughout his life.
- Dramatics activities can put the child in charge of his own learning.

Dramatics activities — carefully chosen and skilfully directed — can be meaningful, relevant, creative experiences that will permanently enrich the minds and imaginations of your pupils. (Forgive me if these terms sound lofty. I believe them.)

Suggestions on using dramatics activities in the classroom are given in the Teacher's Guide, beginning on page 121.

I feel the traditional "putting-on-a-play" approach fails in several ways. Most important, it's largely a non-creative activity. Why should children memorize words somebody else has made up, when they are capable of inventing wonderful words of their own? Why should children follow a teacher's directions on how and when and where to move and speak, when they're able to decide such things for themselves?

There are other objections. Putting on a play is largely a non-democratic activity. Many children don't participate at all. Even if all of the children wanted to participate, usually only three or four get to play "leading" rôles.

Putting on a play generally has, as its objective, entertaining an audience — which means the children must meet performance criteria that are not their own. By and large, I think children should take part in dramatics for their own entertainment, not to amuse their parents or other classes of children.

Putting on a play requires the expenditure of too much effort for the rewards involved. There are rewards involved, as I've suggested above — and there are others I haven't mentioned but will discuss later. But are these rewards great enough to justify the work involved? Too frequently, they are not.

While I'm about the business of attacking the traditional play, let me also crack that old chestnut about "being in plays develops poise." For one thing, the children chosen to play the important rôles are invariably the ones who are already poised; that's why they're chosen. For another, most children in plays come down with nervous stomachs, clammy hands, above normal temperatures, and sudden biological impulses. (However, if for various reasons you feel you must put on a play, you will find some advice on that subject at the end of this book.)

Although this book is mainly intended for students and teachers, the activities presented in it could certainly be used by parents for children's parties at home, or for any adults who are not teachers, but who are responsible at times for channelling the energies of groups of children.

Children love to act. They love to make up stories. They love to pretend they are grown-ups or animals or mythical creatures. They love to do all the things dramatics activities involve. What they don't love to do is perform in accordance with somebody else's demands.

Therein lies the chief difference between the traditional approach to dramatics and the creative approach. And that's what this book, YOU CAN ACT!, is all about.

1. Acting in Pantomime

One of the simplest kinds of acting is called *pantomime*. In pantomime, you act silently. You act with your face, with your hands, with your whole body. But you don't say any words. You don't sing or hum. You don't even make noises.

Because you don't speak in a pantomime, there are no words to memorize. That's one of the reasons it's so easy to do.

What can you do in pantomime? Just about anything!

Let's start with some everyday actions, just to practice. Here's a list of ideas. Pick an item from the list (or make up one of your own) and see if you can act it out in such a way that everyone watching will know just what you are doing.

But remember: NO TALKING!

■ Act out how you make your bed and put away your pajamas in the morning.

■ Act out how you take a shower or bath.

■ Act out how you yawn and stretch when you're very tired.

■ Act out how you watch a television show. See if the people watching you can guess from your expressions what kind of show you are watching.

■ Act out how you get breakfast ready. See if the people watching you can guess from the way you use your hands what kind of food you are preparing.

■ Act out how it feels to have a great big sneeze coming on.

■ Act out how you play with your pet. Can the audience guess what kind of pet you have from the way you play with it?

All of those pantomimes were actions you are used to doing. Now add some imagination to your pantomimes. Here are some ideas you might like. In each mime, you have to pretend to be somebody else. Try to imagine what it would feel like to be that person. How would he behave? Can the audience tell from your pantomime what kind of person you are acting? Try and see.

- Be a cowboy riding in a rodeo.
- Be a tight-rope walker in a circus.
- Be a baby learning how to walk.
- Be a blind man, walking down the street, using a cane to guide himself.
- Be a detective, looking for clues.
- Be a policeman, directing traffic.
- Be a ballet dancer on the stage.
- Be an Olympic diving champion.
- Be a taxi driver, making his way through heavy traffic at rush hour. Pretend you have a taxi full of noisy passengers.
- Be a fisherman, or a shoe repairman, or a fireman, or a gardener, or a nurse, or a barber, at work.

You can even be an animal in a pantomime, if you like. See if you can act out these animals in such a way that everyone will know just what kind of animal you are.

- A fish swimming through a pond.
- A cat sneaking up on a mouse.
- A dog eating his dinner.
- A kitten playing with a ball of yarn.
- A bear looking for honey.
- A bloodhound on the scent of something important.
- A bird flying through the treetops.
- A horse trying to throw his rider.
- A bull spotting a stranger in his field.
- A rooster giving the first crow of the day. (Remember to do it silently!)
- A hen hatching a nest of eggs.
- A fox sneaking up on a goose.

For that last idea, you might like to use someone else in your pantomime. One of you can be the fox while the other one is the goose.

13

Here are more ideas for pantomimes using more than one actor. Some of them are about animals and some are about people. Some are serious and some are silly. But all of them can be lots of fun to do — and lots of fun to watch. Try them.

- You and your friend get caught in the rain.
- You and your friend have a game of tennis.
- You and your friend have a swimming race.
- A bullfighter meets a bull.
- Two donkeys go dancing together.
- Two turtles have a race.
- You and your friend have a tug-of-war. Don't use a real rope. Act it out as though you had a rope, and try to "feel" the imaginary rope in your hands. When someone at one side of the rope pulls, what happens to the person on the other side?
- Two elephants walk a tightrope. The elephants carry parasols in their trunks to help them balance.
- Two giraffes have a tea party.
- Two dogs meet each other for the first time.
- You and your friend have a race — on stilts.
- Two bears have a race — on stilts.
- You and your friend, rowing separate boats, crash into each other.
- Two kangaroos have a boxing match.
- A snake-charmer performs with a cobra.
- A child plays with a puppy.
- A cowboy ropes a bucking bronco.

Did you ever wonder, "What would happen if . . . ?" Here are some pantomimes you can do that will help you find the answers.

14

- What would happen if you heard the world's funniest joke?
- What would happen if you had the world's biggest sneeze?
- What would happen if you read the world's saddest story?
- What would happen if you watched the world's most boring television show?
- What would happen if your legs suddenly turned into sponge-rubber?
- What would happen if the world suddenly turned into candy, cake, and ice cream?
- What would happen if monkeys played basketball or football?
- What would happen if dinosaurs danced?
- What would happen if elephants jumped rope?
- What would happen if hippopotamuses climbed coconut trees?
- What would happen if birds flew backward?
- What would happen if you went into a dark cave where you couldn't see anything — and a strange animal was in the cave? What kind of animal is it? How can you tell he's there? Are you brave or frightened? Maybe he's more afraid of you than you are of him. Act it out, and show us what would happen!

Now that you've had some practice doing pantomimes, you and your friends can work together to tell a whole story in pantomime. Here's how to do it.

First, read the ideas given below. Then, divide up the parts, so that there is someone to play each person or animal in the story. Practice each action in the story until you are satisfied with it. Then, put all the separate pieces of action together in order, and practice the whole story. When it is as good as you can make it, it's time to perform it for an audience. Your classmates are a good audience. At home, you can do the pantomime for your parents, your brothers, and your sisters.

Let's begin with some well-known nursery rhymes. You can make a guessing game out of this, if you like, by having the audience guess, after each one, just which nursery rhyme you were doing.

Little Miss Muffet

> Little Miss Muffet
> Sat on a tuffet,
> Eating some curds and whey.
> Along came a spider
> Who sat down beside her,
> And frightened Miss Muffet away.

First, Miss Muffet comes in, carrying her supper. Is it in a bowl, or on a tray? You decide.

She looks around for a comfortable place to sit. She decides to sit on the tuffet. (You may not know what a "tuffet" is in real life, so you will have to decide what it might be. A chair? A low stool? A clump of grass?) Perhaps the tuffet is dusty, and Miss Muffet must clean it before she sits down. Will she dust it with her apron? With her pocket handkerchief? Will she blow the dust off? You decide — then act it out.

When the tuffet is clean, Miss Muffet sits down, makes herself comfortable, and begins to eat her curds and whey. Does she eat with her fingers, or with a spoon?

Suddenly, the spider enters. What kind of fellow do you think he might be? Show the audience by the way you act.

He sees Miss Muffet — but she doesn't see him. Slowly . . . slowly . . . he approaches. Suddenly, Miss Muffet realizes she is not alone. How does that happen? Perhaps the spider taps her on the shoulder. Or maybe she senses someone is there and turns around. You decide how it happens, and act it out.

Miss Muffet is surprised! She throws up her hands in horror. She jumps up. What happens then? Perhaps the spider

just wants to be friends. If that's the case, he might bow low to her, as though saying "How do you do?" Or perhaps he is a mean spider, and really wants to frighten her away. In that case, how would he do it? Act it out.

In any case, Miss Muffet is so frightened that she runs away. What does the spider do then? If he is a mean spider, he might laugh at Miss Muffet's fright. If he is a friendly spider, he might sit down on the tuffet himself and give a lonely sigh. You see, what he does depends on what kind of spider you decide to make him.

But no matter what kind of spider he is, it isn't likely that he'd let good curds and whey go to waste. So at the end of the pantomime, he would probably begin to eat Miss Muffet's supper himself.

The Queen of Hearts

The Queen of Hearts
She made some tarts,
All on a summer's day;
The Knave of Hearts
He stole the tarts,
And took them clean away.
The King of Hearts
Called for the tarts,
And beat the Knave full sore;
The Knave of Hearts
Brought back the tarts,
And vowed he'd steal no more.

The scene is the Royal Kitchen. It is a warm summer's day. The Queen of Hearts sits in a chair, and waits for the tarts to finish baking. She might mop her brow with her handkerchief. Or perhaps she fans her face with her hand. She peeks into the oven. No — the tarts aren't quite ready yet. Perhaps she taps her foot as she waits, which shows that she is impatient. Now she opens the oven door again. Good! She sees the tarts are ready.

Using pot-holders, she removes the tarts from the oven. She carries the pan to the table where she carefully sets it down. She sniffs at the tarts. How good they smell! She begins to remove the tarts from the pan to a plate.

But the Queen is not alone. Someone has just come into the kitchen. It is the Knave of Hearts. He smells something — something good. He licks his lips. He pats his tummy. His eyes light up. He wants those tarts!

How will he get them? Will he boldly rush up and snatch the plate away, right before the Queen's eyes? Or will he wait until her back is turned, and then sneak up on tiptoe and steal the tarts as quickly as he can? Perhaps he decides to trick the Queen. In that case, he might go right up to her boldly as she works, and start a conversation (in pantomime, of course). He could admire her dress — and as she turns around to show it off to him, he could steal the tarts.

What does he do with the stolen tarts? Does he stuff them into his pockets and then try to look innocent? Or does he grab the whole plateful and run out of the room with them?

Now, here comes the King. He, too, stops at the doorway and sniffs the air. My, but those tarts smell good! He indicates to the Queen that he would like one of the tarts to eat. She smiles happily, and goes to the table to get him one. Horrors! The tarts are gone!

The King comes to see what the Queen is crying about. She points to the table where the tarts were. Gone! What is to be done? The King walks back and forth, thinking. What could have happened to the tarts? Suddenly, he has an idea.

He calls for the Knave of Hearts. If the Knave ran out of the room, the King must go to the door to call for him. If the Knave is standing innocently in the kitchen, the King need only sternly point his finger at him. In either case, the King accuses the Knave of stealing the tarts.

Does the Knave admit it at once? Or does he try to pretend he doesn't know anything about the tarts? How does the truth come out? Perhaps the King reaches into the Knave's pocket and finds a tart. Or maybe the Queen discovers the truth by noticing jam on the Knave's face. You decide.

Now the King must beat the Knave. He could pantomime slapping his hands. Or he could pantomime hitting him on the back with a mixing spoon or his sword. Or he could pantomime giving him a spanking. Certainly the Knave will burst into tears and beg the King to stop.

The King wants to be sure the Knave will never steal again. The Knave nods his head quickly up and down. He crosses his heart that he will be good from now on. He even gives back the rest of the stolen tarts.

So the King forgives him. So does the Queen. They both shake hands with the Knave. At the end of the pantomime, the three can sit down happily at the kitchen table, and begin to eat the tarts.

Here are some more nursery rhymes to act out in pantomime. Now that you know how to do it, you can turn them into pantomimes all by yourself.

Mary Had a Little Lamb

Mary had a little lamb,
   Its fleece was white as snow;
And everywhere that Mary went
   The lamb was sure to go.
It followed her to school one day.
   That was against the rule.
It made the children laugh and play,
   To see a lamb in school.

Tweedledum and Tweedledee

Tweedledum and Tweedledee
  Agreed to fight a battle,
For Tweedledum said Tweedledee
  Had spoiled his nice new rattle.
Just then flew by a monstrous crow,
  As black as a tar barrel,
Which frightened both the heroes so,
  They quite forgot their quarrel.

Georgie, Porgie

Georgie Porgie, pudding and pie,
Kissed the girls and made them cry;
When the boys came out to play,
Georgie Porgie ran away.

Tom, Tom, the Piper's Son

Tom, Tom, the piper's son,
Stole a pig and away did run;
The pig was eat, and Tom was beat,
Till he ran crying down the street.

Of course, nursery rhymes aren't the only things you can act out in pantomime. Here are some ideas for other pantomimes you can do.

A Snowball Battle in Pantomime

It's a cold winter morning, after a snowfall. The scene is the back yard of a house in the suburbs.

First, several boys and girls come into the yard to play. They run and jump in the snow, and slide about, just having a good time.

Then they decide to build a snowman. First, they make a great big ball of snow for the bottom. They put another ball of snow on top of that. Then they put a smaller ball on top, for the head. Perhaps one of the boys decides to put his own cap on the snowman's head. When the snowman is finished, the boys and girls look at him and like the way he looks. Then they all join hands and dance around the snowman in delight.

Now what can they play? Someone has an idea. They can have a snowball fight. Quickly, they divide up into teams. Maybe it will be the boys against the girls. Or maybe there will be both boys and girls on each team. You decide.

Each team goes to its side of the yard. Everyone starts to make snowballs as fast as possible. Now the fight begins! They all begin tossing the snowballs as fast as they can make them. They take aim at those on the other team. Sometimes the snowballs miss their mark. Sometimes somebody gets hit with a snowball. How does it feel to get hit with a cold, wet snowball? How do you brush off the snow? Act it out! Everyone is laughing in excitement.

And then — the sun comes out! Perhaps a boy or girl can take the part of the sun and come dancing in. How would the sun move about? Or perhaps the boys and girls just look up in the sky as they feel the sun.

The sun gets warmer and warmer. The boys and girls get warmer and warmer. They unbutton the top buttons on their coats. They take their mittens off and stuff them into their pockets.

Look! The snowman is melting! All the children run to the snowman and stand around him, watching him melt. Perhaps someone would like to take the part of the snowman here, and pantomime how a snowman melts. He's melting — he's melting! The boy who gave the snowman his hat takes it back and puts it back on his own head. But the hat is cold and wet, so he quickly takes it off again and rubs his head to dry off.

The snowman is all melted away. No more snowman! No

more snowball fight! All the boys and girls go off to find another game they can play.

A Circus in Pantomime

Let's have a circus in pantomime.

First, the ring-master comes into the ring, and bows to the audience. He cracks his big whip. He points to one side, introducing the first act.

Act a Lion-Tamer

The first act comes in. It is a lion-taming act. There is a boy to play the lion-tamer. There is a girl to play his assistant. There are three lions (who walk around bent over, not on hands and knees). The lion-tamer carries a whip. The assistant carries a chair.

First, the lion-tamer directs one lion to climb up on the chair and sit there nicely. Then he directs the other two lions to sit on their haunches, one on either side of the chair. He cracks his whip as a signal. At the signal, the three lions all throw their heads back and put their paws up in front of their chests. When the lion-tamer cracks his whip again, the trick is over. The lions prowl about the ring.

For the next trick, the lion-tamer and his assistant make the three lions form a straight line, one behind the other. He cracks his whip, and each lion puts his forepaws on the shoulders of the lion in front of him. The front lion puts his paws up in a begging position, and all three lions rise onto their hind legs. The lion-tamer cracks his whip. The trick is over and the lions go prowling about the ring once more.

For the last trick, the assistant leads two lions to one sidé. She makes them lie down and be still, and she keeps one hand on each of their collars. Then the lion-tamer leads the third lion to the chair. He makes the lion put his forepaws on the seat of the chair. Then the lion-tamer cracks his whip. The lion opens his mouth — very, very wide. Slowly, the lion-tamer pretends to put his head into the lion's mouth. This is a very dangerous trick. The lion-tamer is nervous, but he must try to act calm. The other two lions may become restless as they watch this trick, but the assistant quiets them down. At last, the lion-tamer's head is in! Slowly, slowly, he pulls it back out of the lion's mouth. He smiles broadly. He cracks his whip. The three lions line up together, with the assistant at one end and the lion-tamer at the other. They all bow to the audience and go running off.

Act a Tight-Rope Walker

The ring-master comes in from the other side of the stage. He leads a beautiful girl by the hand. The girl carries a parasol. The ring-master and the girl bow to each other. The ring-master goes out.

The girl is a tight-rope walker. The tight-rope is an imaginary line across the middle of the circus ring. The girl opens her parasol, and runs to one end of the tight-rope. Carrying the parasol over her head to help her balance, the girl very slowly and carefully begins to walk the tight-rope. She puts one foot directly in front of the other. She takes another tiny step. And another. When she reaches the middle of the tight-rope, she begins to sway a bit. She must use her arms carefully to balance herself. When she has regained her balance, she starts to walk once more. Quickly, lightly, she walks to the end of the tight-rope. She made it! She smiles happily, gives a little jump, and bows to the audience. Then she goes running out.

Act a Clown

Here come the clowns! There are at least four of them. It is their job to make the audience laugh. They perform all sorts of stunts. They may turn cart-wheels or somersaults. One may bend down on all fours behind another clown; then a third clown can push the standing one over backward. The clowns walk in a silly way. They wave at the audience. They smile all the time. Then they all bow low and go running off.

Other Acts

The circus can have more acts if you like. Is there someone who wants to be a dancing bear? Is there someone who wants to be a snake-charmer? Perhaps three or four boys and girls would like to be circus ponies. Or maybe someone wants to pantomime being a sword-swallower. Your circus can have as many pantomime acts as you like. Some actors can be in more than one act. At the beginning of each act, the ring-master presents the performer to the audience. At the end of each act, the performers bow low to the audience.

After the last act, end the circus with a grand parade around the ring. All the performers, including the animals, walk in a big circle, once around the ring, waving to the audience and smiling happily. The ring-master leads the parade. When he reaches the spot where everyone will go out, he stands aside as the rest of the parade marches off. Then he bows grandly to the audience. The circus is over.

What else would make a good pantomime? A bullfight? An Olympic Games competition, with many different sports represented? Santa Claus and his elves and reindeer getting ready for Christmas Eve? You'll think of lots of good pantomimes to do. When you do — act them out!

Acting Out Longer Stories

Now that you've acted out some short rhymes and situations in pantomime, you may want to act out longer stories. For these, you will want to have a reader. The reader will stand at the side of the room and read the story aloud. As he reads, the others in the group will act out the story in pantomime.

Practicing the pantomime itself is the most important part.

And, of course, the reader will want to practice his reading aloud by himself. But it is also important to practice putting the two parts together. That way, the reader will leave enough pauses for the action.

A good story to start with is "Hansel and Gretel." In addition to the reader, you will need five actors: one to be Hansel, one to be Gretel, one to be the Mother, one to be the Father, and one to be the Witch.

Hansel and Gretel

(The first scene is in the cottage. There are a table and chairs. There is a cupboard. There is a door to the outside. At the beginning of the pantomime, Hansel is sitting in a chair, working at making brooms. Gretel is knitting a stocking.)

Reader: Once upon a time, there was a boy named Hansel and a girl named Gretel. They lived with their mother and father in a cottage at the edge of a wood. They were very poor, and hardly had enough to eat. So they were always hungry.

One day, when they were alone in the cottage, Hansel decided he was too hungry to work.

(Hansel throws down his broom, gets up, and scowls. He puts his arms around his empty stomach and bends over slightly to show how hungry he is.)

Reader: "I'm too hungry to go on making brooms," said Hansel. Gretel was shocked. "You should be ashamed of yourself, Hansel," she cried.

(Gretel shakes her finger at Hansel.)

Reader: But Hansel didn't care. He was hungry — hungry — hungry! And how can you work when all you can think about is food?

(Hansel stamps around the room, kicking the broom out of his way.)

Reader: Gretel, however, just smiled. "If you promise to be good, Hansel," she said, "I'll tell you a secret."

(Hansel stops stamping and looks at Gretel in surprise. Gretel signals "Come here" to him with her finger, and he goes to her.)

Reader: "When Mother comes home," said Gretel, "she will make us a rice pudding for supper. She has a whole pitcher of cream that she has been saving for it." But Hansel didn't believe his sister.

(Hansel gestures "Oh, go on with you!" at Gretel and turns his back.)

Reader: "It's really true!" said Gretel. "Look, and I'll show you."

(Hansel turns back. Gretel gets up and goes to the cupboard. She opens the cupboard and takes down a pitcher of cream, which she carries to the table and sets down. Hansel, his eyes wide with delight, follows her.)

Reader: "See?" said Gretel. "What did I tell you?"

(Hansel sticks his finger into the pitcher and tastes the cream by licking off his finger.)

Reader: Mmm! Sweet, rich, cream! "Now let's get back to our work," said Gretel. "I must finish knitting this stocking before Mother comes home, and you must finish making your broom." But Hansel didn't want to work. He wanted to play.

(Gretel goes back to her chair and goes on with her knitting. Hansel folds his arms to show that he doesn't want to work. Gretel shakes her finger at him.)

Reader: "Work's no fun," said Hansel. "Let's dance instead."

(He goes to Gretel and tries to take her hands. She pushes him away, and starts to knit. He grabs for her again. This time she looks up at him. He smiles at her. She smiles back, puts down her knitting, and takes his hands. They start dancing around the room gaily.)

27

Reader: So Hansel and Gretel began to dance about. Suddenly, the door opened. Mother was home!

(Mother comes in. She is horrified at what she sees. Puts her hands on her hips and scowls. Hansel and Gretel stop dancing at once. They look at Mother with fear. Mother shakes her finger at them.)

Reader: "What's this?" cried Mother. "Dancing and singing when you should be working!"

(Gretel quickly goes back to her seat and begins knitting. Hansel crosses his arms and stands firmly where he is.)

Reader: Mother was very angry. "It's a whipping for you, Hansel!" she cried. Mother reached for the whip, and began to chase Hansel about the room. "Just wait till I catch you," she cried.

(Mother, whip in hand, chases Hansel round and round. Finally, she reaches across the table to grab him, and in so doing, knocks the pitcher to the floor.)

Reader: Crash!

(Mother and Hansel both stop and stare at the pitcher. Gretel jumps up and stares, too.)

Reader: The pitcher had fallen off the table, and all the lovely cream was spilled. Mother was *really* angry. "See what you have done," she cried. "Now there is nothing left for our supper!" And Mother began to cry.

(Mother sits beside the table, her face in her hands, weeping. Hansel and Gretel go to her to comfort her.)

Reader: "I'm sorry, Mother," said Gretel. "We didn't mean it," said Hansel.

(Mother looks up angrily.)

Reader: "Being sorry is all well and good," said Mother. "But what are we to do about supper?" Then Gretel had an idea. "I know!" she cried.

(Gretel smiles brightly. She darts to the cupboard, takes a basket from it, and brings it back to Mother and Hansel.)

Reader: "Hansel and I will get supper," cried Gretel. "We'll take this basket into the woods and pick wild strawberries." "Hurrah!" cried Hansel. It was a wonderful idea.

(Hansel claps his hands, smiles, and jumps up and down.)

Reader: And before Mother could say a word, off went Hansel and Gretel with the basket.

(Hansel and Gretel run out hand in hand, as Mother looks after them in surprise.)

Reader: "Perhaps they're not such bad children after all," thought Mother to herself.

(Mother smiles and nods.)

Reader: Soon, Father came home. "Hello, Mother," he cried.

(Father comes in, smiling broadly. He comes to Mother and puts his hand on her shoulder. Then he puts his hand under her chin and raises her face so that he may look at it. He frowns.)

Reader: "But, Mother," exclaimed Father. "You've been crying." "Look!" said Mother. "All the cream I was saving for supper is spilled. Those children of ours!"

(Mother gets up, goes to where the cream is spilled, and points. Father shakes his head sadly. Then he looks about, puzzled.)

Reader: "But where *are* the children?" asked Father. "They've gone to the woods to pick strawberries," said Mother.

(Mother points out the door. Father is horrified and seizes Mother's hand.)

Reader: "Oh, no!" cried Father. "We must go after them and bring them home!" "Why?" asked Mother. "Have you forgotten the wicked witch who lives in the woods?" he cried. "Come, Mother, come. We must find the children and bring them home before anything happens to them. We must find Hansel and Gretel!"

(Father goes rushing out the door, and Mother goes rushing out after him.)

Reader: Of course, Hansel and Gretel didn't know anything about a wicked witch. All they knew was that it was their fault there was no cream, and they had made up their minds to pick a whole basketful of wild strawberries. And so into the woods they went, carrying their basket between them. Picking berries is hard work, but Hansel and Gretel didn't mind. Deeper, deeper, deeper into the woods they wandered, picking wild strawberries all the while.

(As the Reader has been reading this part of the story, someone moves the furniture from the cottage scene out of the way. In its place, the Witch's house is set up. There is also a cage at one side and a big oven at the other side. Chairs may be used to represent the door to the Witch's house, the door to the cage, and the door to the oven.)

Reader: Before they knew it, Hansel and Gretel had come to a part of the woods they had never seen before.

(Hansel and Gretel come in from one side and look all about them.)

Reader: "Where are we, Hansel?" asked Gretel. "I'm not sure," said Hansel. "But look! There's a house!"

(Hansel points to the Witch's house.)

Reader: "Why don't we knock at the door and ask the people who live there how we can find our way home?" So Hansel and Gretel began to move toward the little house they had found. Suddenly, they stopped. They couldn't believe their eyes! They had never seen a house like this before! It was made out of cake and candy and gingerbread, and covered with good things to eat!

(Hansel and Gretel look at each other, not daring to believe their eyes. They smile broadly at one another. Then they run to the house and begin breaking off pieces of it which they stuff into their mouths.)

Reader: How good it all tasted! Hansel and Gretel just ate, and ate, and ate. Suddenly, they heard a noise. It came from inside the house. It was a strange noise. A frightening noise.

(Hansel and Gretel look at each other, afraid. They run away from the house and huddle together, their arms about each other, staring at the door of the house. Then the Witch comes out of the house.)

Reader: An old woman came out of the house. She was the ugliest woman Hansel and Gretel had ever seen. But the old woman smiled so nicely at them, and seemed so friendly, that the children forgot to be afraid.

(Witch smiles and waves to the children to come to her. They approach her — timidly at first, then more boldly. The Witch gestures as though to say, "Come, and eat as much as you like." Hansel and Gretel happily begin nibbling at the house once more.)

Reader: But the old woman wasn't as nice as she pretended to be. And when the children weren't looking, she crept up behind Hansel and seized him. Before he knew what was happening, the old woman had thrust him into a cage and locked the door.

(Witch tiptoes up behind Hansel, seizes him from behind, pinning his arms to his side, then drags him to the cage. She pushes him in, slams the door, and with a key that hangs on a chain at her belt, locks the door.)

Reader: "Let me out! Let me out!" cried Hansel, and he beat his fists on the cage. But the wicked old Witch just laughed. Then she turned to Gretel.

*(Hansel beats on cage. Witch throws back her head and laughs loudly —
in pantomime, of course. Then she turns and begins walking toward
Gretel. Gretel shivers and pulls away, moving backward as the Witch
comes closer.)*

Reader: "What — what are you doing with my brother?"
asked Gretel. "I'm going to bake him in my oven, until he's
turned into gingerbread," said the Witch. "But first, you must
look into the oven to see if it is hot enough."

*(Witch gestures toward oven door. Gretel shakes her head "No," and
shrugs her shoulders, opening her palms outward.)*

Reader: "I don't know how to test the oven," said Gretel.
"Perhaps if you show me how, then I can do it." "It's very
simple," said the Witch. "You just open the door and bend
way over, like this."

*(Witch opens oven door and bends way over into it. Gretel quickly
snatches the cage key from the Witch's belt. Just as the Witch stands
upright and turns to face her, Gretel hides the key behind her back.)*

Reader: "Were you watching closely?" asked the Witch.

(Gretel shakes her head "No.")

Reader: "I'm so foolish," said Gretel. "You were much too
quick for me. Please show me again. But do it very slowly this
time, so I'll be sure to learn." "Very well," said the Witch.
"I'll show you one more time. You put your head in, just like
this."

*(Witch begins to show her how it's done once more, doing it all very
slowly. As soon as the Witch's back is turned, Gretel runs to the cage
and unlocks it, letting Hansel out. Then together the children tiptoe up
behind the Witch and give her a big push.)*

Reader: Bang! Before she knew what had happened, the old
Witch had been pushed into the oven by Hansel and Gretel.
Quickly they slammed the oven door.

(Witch falls forward into oven. Hansel and Gretel hold door closed.)

Reader: Then Hansel and Gretel hugged each other. What a narrow escape they had had!

(Children give great sighs of relief. Mother and Father come running in.)

Reader: Just then, Mother and Father arrived. How happy they were to find Hansel and Gretel. And how happy Hansel and Gretel were to see Mother and Father!

(They all hug one another. Then all join hands and begin skipping and dancing about in a circle.)

Reader: The Witch, of course, was never heard from again. And from that day on, whenever Hansel and Gretel were too hungry to work, they just ate another piece of the Witch's wonderful gingerbread house. And Hansel and Gretel and Mother and Father lived happily ever after.

(Hansel, Gretel, Mother and Father all go running up to the Witch's house and begin munching pieces of it, smiling broadly.)

The End

Making Up Parts of a Story Yourself

Here's another story to act out in pantomime as a reader stands at one side, reading aloud. But this story is a special story. You must decide some very important things about it before you can act it out in pantomime.

The story is about someone named Pippy and someone named Diddy. But just who or what are Pippy and Diddy? Are they two boys, or two girls, or a boy and a girl? Or are they animals of some kind — mice, perhaps, or moles, or kangaroos? Or perhaps they are make-believe creatures, like elves or fairies or gnomes.

And who, or what, are Grinkle, Grankle, and Groo? These are questions you must decide before you are ready to begin to act the pantomime.

You must also decide just what the surprise in the story is. When you have decided, the way you act will tell the audience what the surprise is. Maybe it is something to eat. Maybe it is something to wear. Maybe it is a toy. Or maybe it is something else. You decide.

Pippy and Diddy Get a Surprise

(The scene is a woodland clearing. A stream is at one side.)

Reader: Once upon a time, Pippy and Diddy lived in a beautiful little house in a green, green wood. They lived all alone, with no one to tell them what to do. Sometimes they slept, and sometimes they took care of their beautiful little house. But most of the time, they played and played in the green, green wood.

(Pippy and Diddy come in, and begin to play. What shall they play? Hide and seek? Jump rope? Catch? Or do they just dance about gaily? You decide what would be fun for them to do.)

Reader: One day, as Pippy and Diddy were playing, Pippy suddenly thought of something. It was such an important thought, Pippy stopped playing, and stood very still.

(Pippy gets an idea and stands still, deep in thought. Diddy looks on, wondering what Pippy is doing.)

Reader: "Whatever are you doing, Pippy?" asked Diddy. "I'm thinking about what day today is," answered Pippy. "And what day is today?" asked Diddy. "It's our birthday," replied Pippy. "And I think we ought to have a birthday party, this very minute."

(Pippy has been talking to Diddy in pantomime, nodding his head and wagging his finger. Now both smile. Diddy jumps up and down in delight.)

Reader: "That's a wonderful idea," said Diddy. "You call all our friends, while I find things to eat." So right then and there, they began to get ready for the party. While Pippy went to invite their friends —

(Pippy goes off, waving "Goodbye" to Diddy, who waves back.)

Reader: Diddy made the preparations. First, there were berries to pick. Then, there was water to fetch from the stream to make tea. Fortunately, there was an old hollowed-out tree branch lying on the ground, just the right size to carry water in.

(Diddy picks berries, then picks up the branch and goes to one side to fill it with water from the stream.)

Reader: Then Diddy decided to gather some flowers for the party, and to look for some wild honey. Hurrah! In a tree nearby was plenty of honey — enough to serve all the guests.

(Diddy gathers flowers, then looks into trees for honey. At the third tree, Diddy sees the honey, and smiles and jumps with joy. Then Diddy gathers the honey and brings it to the place where the other things are. What would make a good table? The ground? A tree stump? A fallen log? You decide.)

Reader: Just as Diddy finished making all the preparations, Pippy returned, bringing the guests for the party. The guests were Pippy and Diddy's three very best friends. First, there was Grinkle.

(Pippy comes in with Grinkle.)

Reader: "Happy Birthday, Diddy! Happy Birthday, Pippy!" said Grinkle, and they all shook hands.

(Everybody shakes hands. Then, Grankle comes in.)

Reader: The second friend to arrive was Grankle, who had taken extra pains to look neat and clean, because it was a party. "Happy Birthday, Diddy! Happy Birthday, Pippy!" cried Grankle, and they all shook hands.

(Everybody shakes hands again. Then Groo comes in, carrying something behind his back.)

Reader: Last to arrive was Groo. Groo was *always* the last to arrive. "Happy Birthday, Diddy! Happy Birthday, Pippy!" cried Groo. But Groo did *not* shake hands — because Groo was carrying something. "What have you behind your back?" asked Pippy. "What are you hiding?" asked Diddy. "It's a secret," said Groo. "It's a special secret. It's a special secret surprise." Diddy and Pippy looked at one another. What could the special secret surprise be? They looked at their guests. Grinkle was smiling. Grankle was smiling. Groo was smiling. At last, Grinkle said, "Oh, show them the surprise, Groo."

(Grinkle and Grankle, smiling, push Groo forward. Groo holds out the package he has been hiding. Pippy and Diddy's eyes light up with surprise and delight. Groo bows low and he presents the package, and Grinkle and Grankle bow low, too.)

Reader: "Thank you, thank you," cried Pippy and Diddy. "Oh, what can it be?" "Open it and see," said Grinkle. "Shall I open it, Pippy, or will you?" asked Diddy. "Let's open it together," said Pippy. So Pippy and Diddy opened the surprise birthday present — and what a wonderful surprise it was!

(Pippy and Diddy pantomime opening box as others crowd around, looking on. When the box is open, Pippy and Diddy clap their hands in delight, and take the present out of the box.)

Reader: "What a wonderful present!" said Diddy. "It's just what we wanted!" said Pippy. "Is it the right size?" asked Grinkle. "Is it the right shape?" asked Grankle. "Is it really and truly just what you wanted?" asked Groo. "It really and truly *is*!" exclaimed Diddy and Pippy. And to prove it, they took their present and began to use it right then and there. The three friends joined in, and before you could say Flibberty-gibbet, the green, green wood was ringing with the happy sounds of the best birthday party that ever was.

(All five begin to use the present, and are happily smiling.)

The End

Other Stories to Act Out

There are many stories that would make good pantomimes, especially if you have a good reader to read them aloud. If you like, ask your teacher to help you find more stories and poems to act out in pantomime.

You might want to try stories that are written in verse, like *Wynken, Blynken, and Nod* by Eugene Field, or *A Visit from St. Nicholas* by Clement Moore. Or you might like to pantomime a scene from *Alice in Wonderland* or *A Christmas Carol* while a reader reads aloud.

Or best of all — you might like to make up a story of your very own. Pantomimes to stories you write yourself are probably the most fun of all!

2. Putting In the Words

So far, your acting has been in pantomime. You've acted with your face and with your body. You've acted with your arms and with your legs. Now, it's time to start acting with words, too.

When people act with words, the words they use are called *dialogue* (di-ah-log). You can make up your own dialogue, or you can memorize the dialogue somebody else has written. In this part of the book, you will find acting games that call for both kinds of dialogue.

You can even have dialogue without any words at all. Making sounds with your mouth is a kind of dialogue. Since it is, perhaps, the most fun of all, let's start with that.

Acting a Storm at Sea

First, for practice, act as if you are the wind. We can hear the wind — but wind doesn't say any words. What kinds of sounds does the wind make?

Try making wind sounds of different kinds. Make gentle wind sounds, like a summer breeze. Then make fierce wind sounds, like a hurricane wind.

While one actor is making the sounds of wind, a second may like to make the sounds of booming thunder. A third can make the sharp, crackling sound that sometimes is heard with lightning. Perhaps someone will want to try making the sounds of waves at sea. And someone else can make the sounds of some sea bird.

When everybody has practiced his sounds, you can have a regular storm at sea, with everyone making his sounds at once. And the audience will probably know just what is going on — even though nobody has said a word!

A Boy and His Dog

Here is a dialogue between a boy and his dog. The words for the boy are written out, so that the actor playing the boy can read them or memorize and recite them. But the dog's part of the dialogue isn't written out at all. The actor who plays the part of the dog will have to invent his own dialogue. Will he say "Bow wow wow"? Or "Arf arf"? Or "Grrr-row"? He might say different things, all in the same dialogue. It depends on what the dog is trying to say, and how the actor feels.

Jimmy and Fido

Jimmy (calling for his dog): Fido! Fido! Here, dog!

Fido (comes running in, barks as if to say, "Hello, Jimmy.")

Jimmy (pats dog kindly): Good dog. Good Fido.

Fido (growls as if to say, "I like being patted.")

Jimmy: Let's play a game, Fido. Shall we?

Fido (barks as if to say, "That's a good idea.")

Jimmy: What game shall we play? Shall we play Fetch-the-stick?

Fido (growls as if to say, "No, I'm too tired for that.")

Jimmy: Shall we play with my new rubber ball?

Fido (growls as if to say, "I'm too tired for that, too.")

Jimmy: I know! Let's see if we can find some other boys and their dogs to play with.

Fido (barks happily, as if to say, "I'm never too tired to play with other dogs. That's a great idea, Jimmy!")

Jimmy (as he starts to go out): Yes, I thought you'd like that idea. Coming, Fido?

Fido (barks happily, as if to say "I'm right behind you!")

Using Sounds Instead of Words

Here's another dialogue that calls for the actors to make sounds instead of words. Again, the *meaning* of the sounds is given. See if you can make the sounds in such a way that the audience will know just what this funny conversation is all about. (The way you move your body and the expressions on your face will help to make the meaning clear.)

Mrs. Hen and Mr. Rooster

Rooster (crows as if to say, "Good morning, Mrs. Hen.")

Hen (clucks as if to say, "Good morning to you.")

Rooster (crows as if to say, "Don't you look beautiful today!")

Hen (clucks as if to say, "Thank you. My feathers do look nice, if I say so myself.")

Rooster (crows as if to say, "And isn't it a beautiful day!")

Hen (clucks as if to say, "Yes, the sun is shining brightly.")

Rooster (crows as if to say, "Would you like to go for a stroll?")

Hen (clucks as if to say, "Thank you, I think that's a fine idea.")

The trick in making these animal sounds seem like real conversation is to keep changing the way you speak. Some sounds should be loud, some soft. Some sounds should be fast, some slow.

How to Use Words

Even when you are using words instead of just sounds, the way you say the words makes a difference. Here are some words that you would probably say very fast.

— Come quick! Come quick! There's a parade going by!
— I'll be there just as soon as I can.
— Last one in the water is a monkey's uncle!

Here are some words that you would probably say quite slowly.

— I'm so tired, I don't think I can take one more step.
— Aren't we *ever* going to get to Grandma's house?
— I'm telling you for the last time, stay out of my room!

Some words need to be said quite loudly.

— Help! Help! Help!
— Merry Christmas! Merry Christmas!
— Three cheers for the astronauts!

And some words should be said very quietly.

— Don't tell anyone, because it's a secret.
— Please turn down the television set, the baby is sleeping.
— I think this old house may be haunted.

You can tell, just by looking at them, how to say those words. But sometimes, the words themselves don't tell you how they should be said. Then, you have to decide.

Here's a dialogue in which one person just says the same words over and over. But does he say the words the same way each time? How does the actor know how to say the words?

First Actor: Does anybody here like doughnuts?

Second Actor: I like doughnuts for breakfast.

First Actor: How would you like some for lunch?

Second Actor: I like doughnuts for breakfast.

First Actor: For breakfast, I'll bet you like hot dogs.

Second Actor: I like doughnuts for breakfast.

That's a rather silly conversation. But it does show that you can't always tell just from the words themselves the best way to speak those words. You have to figure out what the words mean. Then you can decide which words to make loud, soft, fast, and slow.

Using Words and Actions Together

Now that you've had some practice at speaking dialogue, you can begin putting dialogue together with pantomime. And that's what real acting is all about: words and actions used together to tell a story.

Here is a short story that combines words and actions. All of the words are written out. You can read them out loud, or you can memorize them, and then recite them.

Most of the actions are written out, too, so you will know what to do. But two of the actions are *not* written out. You must decide what those actions are. Each actor will have a different

idea, so try acting this story out several times, with different boys and girls taking the parts.

The Magic Potion

(A witch is stirring something in a kettle. A boy comes in.)

Boy: What are you doing, old witch?

Witch: I'm stirring up a magic potion.

Boy (laughs): Pooh! I don't believe in magic! There's no such thing.

Witch: That's what *you* say. But I'll bet you wouldn't dare *taste* my magic potion.

Boy (a bit afraid): Why? What would happen to me if I tasted it?

Witch: I won't tell you. You'll have to taste it and find out.

Boy (bravely): Ah, that potion business is a fake. I'll taste it, and I'll bet nothing happens.

(The boy takes the witch's stirring spoon and tastes the potion. It is a magic potion. It tastes funny. It makes the boy feel funny. What faces will he make to show how it tastes? What movements will he make to show how it feels? Decide, then act it out.)

Boy: Oh! Oh! It *is* magic. I can feel it! I feel so funny!

(The boy is behaving very strangely as a result of tasting the potion. What is happening to him?)

Boy: Oh! Oh! Make it stop. Oh, please, make it stop. I don't like the way it feels to act this way.

Witch: Now do you believe in magic?

Boy: Yes, yes. Please — make it stop. Help me!

Witch: Very well. I'll do *this* and I'll do *that*!

(What does the witch do when she says "I'll do this"? What does she do when she says "I'll do that"? Does she do something magical with her hands? With her arms? With her whole body? You decide. Whatever it is she does, it works. It takes away the magic spell, and the boy stops behaving strangely.)

Witch: There!

Boy: Ohhh! Thank you. I couldn't have gone on much longer.

Witch: That will teach you not to believe in magic!

If you like, you could change the witch's line about *doing* "this" and "that" to "Very well, I'll say a magic spell." Then, instead of making up actions for her to do, make up words for her to say — magic, marvellous, mysterious words that will make the boy stop behaving strangely.

Making Up Dialogue and Actions

Here's another story in which the actors have to decide what the actions are. But in this story, they have to decide on some of the dialogue, too. That's because the end of the story is not written down. What the actors decide to say and do will decide how the story ends.

The Escape of the Monkeys

(The scene is a zoo. Some monkeys are in a cage, playing. There may be any number of monkeys. How do they play? The boys and girls taking the parts of the monkeys must decide. While the monkeys are playing, two visitors to the zoo come in. They are brother and sister.)

Nancy: Oh, here they are, George. Here are the monkeys.

George (going up to the cage): Hello, monkeys.

Monkeys: Eeek, eeek, eeek!

(What are the monkeys trying to say? You decide.)

Nancy (laughing): Aren't they funny? I wonder what they're saying.

George: I think they're saying, "We're hungry."

Nancy: Maybe they are. They look hungry.

George: Shall I give them some of my peanuts?

Nancy: I don't know, George. I don't think we're supposed to feed the animals.

George: There isn't any sign that *says* "Don't Feed the Animals."

(The monkeys put their hands out through the bars of their cage, as though begging for peanuts.)

Monkeys: Eeek, eeek, eeek!

Nancy: George, I think they *do* want some peanuts.

George: All right, then, I'll give them some.

(He goes over to the monkey cage. When he gets near them, he trips and falls against the cage. The door to the monkey cage flies open.)

Nancy: Oh, George! You've opened the door to their cage!

George (picking himself up from the ground): I did?

(The monkeys are delighted to be free. They rush out of their cage and begin jumping and dancing about.)

Monkeys: Eeek, eeek, eeek, eeek, eeek!

Nancy: Oh, George! What shall we do?

(The monkeys are running all about. What happens next? Can George and Nancy get the monkeys back into their cage? Does anyone

else come along? Who? Does the new person help George and Nancy? Act it out!)

Here are some more stories in which the actors must decide what some of the actions are and what some of the words should be.

The Wolf and the Rabbits

(The scene is a woodland. Mr. Rabbit and Mrs. Rabbit come hopping in. They are in a great hurry, and seem frightened.)

Mr. Rabbit: Hurry, my dear, hurry!

Mrs. Rabbit: I'm coming as fast as I can. But your legs are longer than mine, so you can take bigger hops than I can.

Mr. Rabbit: But there's no time to lose!

Mrs. Rabbit (puffing for breath): No, I just cannot hop another hop. I am too tired. I must rest a minute.

Mr. Rabbit: Very well, my dear. Sit down on this log and catch your breath. But we can only wait the tiniest bit, and then we must hop on.

Mrs. Rabbit (sitting down, fanning her face with her paw): Oh, how good it feels to rest.

(A boy, Nicky, comes in. He is delighted to see the rabbits.)

Nicky: Good afternoon, Mr. Rabbit. Good afternoon, Mrs. Rabbit.

Mr. Rabbit (happily): Nicky! Am I glad to see you!

Mrs. Rabbit: Yes, you're just in time to save us!

Nicky: Save you? What seems to be the trouble?

Mr. Rabbit: It's the wolf. He's after us again. We were

running away, but Mrs. Rabbit got too tired to run any farther. What shall we do? That wolf will catch up with us any minute!

Nicky: Don't worry, Mr. Rabbit. My friends and I will help you.

(Nicky goes to one side and calls his friends.)

Nicky: Say, everybody! Come quick! The rabbits are in trouble, and they need our help.

(Nicky's friends come running in. There may be any number of boys and girls.)

First Friend: What's the trouble?

Second Friend: We'll be glad to help the rabbits.

Nicky: It's the wolf. He's after our friends, and we must stop him.

First Friend: How can we do that?

Nicky: Let's make a wolf trap.

Mrs. Rabbit: A wolf trap?

Mr. Rabbit: How do you make a wolf trap?

Nicky: I'll tell you.

(What kind of trap does Nicky have in mind? How does it work? You decide. Nicky tells his plan to the others, and they set up the trap, just as he tells them. It is up to all the actors to make up words and actions to fit this part of the story. When the trap is finally set up, Nicky speaks again.)

Nicky: There! Our trap is ready!

Mr. Rabbit: And just in time, too. Here comes Mr. Wolf!

A Friend: Do you think the trap will work, Nicky?

Nicky: We'll soon find out.

(Wolf comes running in.)

Wolf: I'll catch you now, you fine, furry rabbits!

(He rushes toward Mr. and Mrs. Rabbit, but he is caught in the trap the children have made.)

Wolf: Help! Help! I'm caught in a trap!

Nicky: And it serves you right, too, Mr. Wolf.

Wolf: What are you going to do with me?

Nicky: We're going to take you to the zoo. You won't be able to make trouble then.

Wolf (happily): The zoo? That's where I've always wanted to live. No more chasing my own food then! I'll live safe and warm in a nice clean cage, and every day at dinner time my food will be brought to me.

Mr. Rabbit: And we rabbits will be safe once more!

All (except Nicky): Hurrah for Nicky! Hurrah for his wonderful wolf trap!

Mr. Higglebee's Robots

(The scene is Mr. Higglebee's workshop. Standing in the middle of the workshop are two robots, Ralph and Roberta. At the beginning of the play, the actors playing the robots must stand very still. Mr. Higglebee is using a screwdriver to tighten screws in the robots' knees. There is a knock at the door.)

Mr. Higglebee (calling out): Come in! Come in!

(Sally and Henry come in.)

Mr. Higglebee: Well, if it isn't my young friends, the Hendersons. Good afternoon, children.

50

Sally: Good afternoon, Mr. Higglebee.

Henry: We came to see what new inventions you've made today.

Mr. Higglebee (proudly): Ah, my friends, today I have created the best invention of my life.

Sally: Better than the sled that doesn't need snow?

Mr. Higglebee: Oh yes, better than that.

Henry: Better than the bed that makes itself each morning?

Mr. Higglebee: Yes, better than that, too. Look!

(He leads Sally and Henry to the robots.)

Sally: What on earth are these?

Henry: They look like a boy and girl all made out of metal.

Mr. Higglebee: These are robots. This is Ralph Robot, and this is Roberta Robot.

Sally: What are robots?

Mr. Higglebee: Robots are mechanical people. By pressing a button, I can make these robots walk. I can make these robots talk. I can make them do anything I want.

Henry (doubtfully): I know you're a good inventor, Mr. Higglebee, but machines that walk and talk? I don't believe it.

Mr. Higglebee: Look. I'll show you. All I have to do is press this button.

(Where is the button that Mr. Higglebee presses? Is it in the back of each robot? Is it on the wall? Is it on a table? You decide.)

Mr. Higglebee: Now, I just tell the robots what I want them to do, and they'll do it.

Sally: Will they do anything at all?

Mr. Higglebee: Watch. Robots, these are my friends, Henry and Sally.

(When Mr. Higglebee talks to them, the robots begin to move. How would robots move? When they speak, what would their voices sound like?)

Roberta: Hello, Sally. I am Roberta Robot.

Ralph: Hello, Henry. I am Ralph Robot.

Henry: Hey! They *can* talk!

Mr. Higglebee: Robots, I want you to clean the workshop.

Robots (speaking together): Yes, Mr. Higglebee.

(The robots begin to clean the workshop. Do they dust? Do they sweep? Do they mop, or empty waste-baskets? You decide — then act it out. After a minute, the robots begin to move faster.)

Sally: Oh dear! I think something is going wrong, Mr. Higglebee.

Henry: The robots are going too fast. Stop them, Mr. Higglebee!

Mr. Higglebee (shouts): Not so fast, Robots! Not so fast. You must work slower.

Ralph: We can't slow down.

Roberta: We must move fast.

Robots (speaking together): Faster and faster and faster!

Sally (excitedly): What will happen, Mr. Higglebee?

Henry: Can't you make them stop?

Mr. Higglebee: I don't know what to do. The robots are out of control. This has never happened before.

Robots (speaking together): Faster and faster and faster!

(Mr. Higglebee tries to get the robots to slow down. How? Does he shout at them? Does he push the starting button? Does he try grabbing them? Perhaps he does all these things, and other things too. But nothing seems to work. The robots keep moving very fast. Finally, the robots just can't go any faster. What happens then? Do they collapse into a heap on the floor? Do they run down gradually, like an engine running out of steam? Do they fall into each other's arms, all tired out? It's up to you to decide.)

Sally (sadly): Poor robots!

Henry: They just couldn't go any faster.

Sally: What will happen now, Mr. Higglebee?

Mr. Higglebee: There's only one thing to be done.

(What does Mr. Higglebee decide? Use your imagination to help Mr. Higglebee decide what to do, so that the play can end.)

The Mysterious Something

Do you remember the pantomime about Pippy and Diddy? You had to decide just who or what they were. You also had to decide about Grinkle, Grankle, and Groo. Did you decide they were children? Or giraffes? Or brownies? Or moles? Or monsters?

Here is a play called "The Mysterious Something" in which you will have to make the same kind of decision. What will the Mysterious Something be? And how will it move? What will it say? And how will its voice sound? It can be fun to decide these things. And it can be extra fun if you decide that the Mysterious Something is quite different from what Pippy and Diddy were. The Mysterious Something should be different from Grinkle, Grankle, and Groo, as well. In fact, maybe it would be best of all if the Mysterious Something were different from anything there has ever been in the whole world!

(The scene is a clearing in the forest. A sign is hanging on a tree. At one side, there is a tree stump sturdy enough to be stood on. A chair can make a good tree stump. Several animals are playing about the clearing. They are a Squirrel, a Rabbit, a Frog, and a Skunk. Suddenly, the Squirrel notices the sign on the tree.)

Squirrel: Look, everybody! There's a sign hanging on this tree.

Frog: A sign? There has never been a sign on that tree before.

Skunk: What does the sign say, Squirrel?

Squirrel: I don't know. I never learned how to read.

Frog: I can't read, either.

Skunk: Neither can I.

Rabbit: I can read! I can read!

Frog: Hooray for Rabbit. Tell us what the sign says, Rabbit.

Rabbit: Let me see. *(In pantomime, Rabbit puts on his glasses and reads the sign quickly to himself.)* Oh dear! Oh dear, oh dear, oh dear!

Skunk: Is it bad news, Rabbit?

Frog: Is it a message from the king?

Squirrel: Is it something dreadful?

Rabbit: (scratching his head): I'm really not sure. It may be good . . .

Others: Hooray!

Rabbit: . . . and it may be bad.

Others (groaning): Ohh.

Rabbit: I'll read it out loud to you, and then you can judge for yourselves.

Squirrel: Let's gather round and sit quietly, everybody, while Rabbit reads the sign.

(Animals sit on the ground around Rabbit, who reads the sign aloud.)

Rabbit: The sign says, "To Whom It May Concern."

Squirrel (nudging Frog and Skunk): That means us.

Rabbit (sternly): Shh! *(Reads aloud.)* "To Whom It May Concern. On Wednesday morning, when the sun is at its highest in the sky, I am coming to the forest. I am coming to the forest to live. If the animals of the forest treat me well, I will be their friend. But if the animals of the forest make me angry, or hurt my feelings, or upset my temper, I shall punish them with a dreadful punishment. I expect all of the animals of the forest to be under this tree to greet me when I arrive. Yours very truly, Mysterious Something."

Squirrel (jumping up): I don't like it. Not one bit. Did you hear that part about a dreadful punishment? I'll bet this Mysterious Something is some kind of giant.

Skunk: He sounds more like a dragon to me. The kind that breathes fire.

Frog: Wait a minute, friends. Did you hear the part about being a good friend? Perhaps the Mysterious Something is gentle and kind. Maybe he's a puppy dog. Or maybe he's a lost boy.

Rabbit: We'll find out soon enough what the Mysterious Something is. The sign says he's coming on Wednesday when the sun is at its highest in the sky.

Squirrel: And today is Wednesday.

Frog (looking up): And look! The sun has almost reached the top of the sky!

Rabbit: Listen, everybody! I think I hear footsteps.

(All the animals are suddenly very quiet, listening.)

Squirrel (squealing): Oh, he's coming, he's coming! The Mysterious Something is coming!

Frog: If only we had some idea of what the Mysterious Something is. If only we had some clue. Then I wouldn't be so frightened.

Rabbit: I know! Perhaps if one of us stood on that tree stump, he might get a glimpse of the Mysterious Something coming through the forest.

Frog: Good idea, Rabbit.

Rabbit: Skunk, you're the tallest. Climb up on the stump and see what you can see.

(The Skunk climbs up on the tree stump and peers off to where the footsteps are coming from.)

Squirrel: Can you see anything?

Skunk (excitedly): Yes, yes! I see the Mysterious Something!

Rabbit: Tell us. What does he look like?

Skunk: All right. Here's how the Mysterious Something looks. . . .

(What does Skunk say? How big does he say the Mysterious Something is? What shape is the Mysterious Something? What is he wearing? How is he walking? Is he making any noise as he walks? Does he look friendly — or does he look frightening? It is up to the actors to decide.)

Skunk (when he has finished describing the Mysterious Something): And look! Here he comes now!

(Skunk points and all the other animals look as the Mysterious Something comes in.)

Animals (bowing): Good afternoon, Mysterious Something.

(Do they say this in a frightened manner, or in a friendly manner? And what is the manner of the Mysterious Something when he answers?)

Mysterious Something: Good afternoon, animals. I see you all read my message.

Squirrel: Oh yes, we did.

Frog: It is a very interesting message.

Rabbit: Most interesting.

Skunk: Only. . . .

Mysterious Something: Only what?

Skunk: Only — it needs a bit of explaining.

Mysterious Something: I thought it was perfectly clear. What can I explain?

Skunk: Well, you ask us not to make you angry. What kinds of things make you angry?

Squirrel: You ask us not to upset your temper. What kinds of things upset your temper?

Rabbit: You ask us not to hurt your feelings. What kinds of things hurt your feelings?

Mysterious Something: Ah! I see what the problem is. Very well, I shall explain. The thing that makes me angriest is. . . . *(What? What does the Mysterious Something say?)* The thing that most upsets my temper is. . . . *(What?)* And the thing that is certain to hurt my feelings is. . . . *(What?)*

Skunk: We promise we will never. . . . *(he mentions the thing that makes the Mysterious Something angry.)* We wouldn't want to make you angry.

Squirrel: We promise we will never. . . . *(he mentions the thing that makes the Mysterious Something lose his temper.)* We wouldn't want to upset your temper.

Rabbit: And we promise we will never. . . . *(he mentions the thing that hurts the Mysterious Something's feelings.)* We wouldn't want to hurt your feelings.

Frog: And most of all, we promise that we will all be your good friends and live in peace with you.

Mysterious Something: If you follow those rules, I'm sure we will all get along just perfectly.

Animals: Welcome to our forest, Mysterious Something! Welcome to our forest!

Making Up All the Words
For a Story to Act Out

Now that you have had some practice in making up words to say while you act, you might like to try making up *all* the words for a short play. Here are some stories to act out. The stories tell you who the characters are. They tell you what happens. But they don't tell you what anybody says. Use your imagination and make up the words as you go along.

The Shoemaker and the Elves

The scene is the shop of a poor shoemaker and his wife. It is late at night, almost time for bed. The shoemaker and his wife talk about how poor they are. The shoemaker shows his wife the one piece of leather he has left. It is only enough to make a single pair of shoes. The shoemaker suggests that he will cut out the shoes before going to bed, but his wife reminds him how late it is. She tells him to leave it until the morning, and gives him good reasons why he should do so. So the shoemaker leaves the piece of leather on his work bench, and the two go off to bed.

As soon as they are gone, a laughing sound is heard. Then, from every direction, a family of elves comes trooping in. They have been hiding in the house. They have heard everything the shoemaker and his wife have said. Because the elves like the old shoemaker and his wife, they decide to help. Quickly they set to work and, almost in the twinkling of an eye, they have turned the piece of leather into a beautiful pair of shoes. When the shoes are finished, the elves go dancing out, laughing happily.

The next morning, when the shoemaker and his wife come into the shop, they can hardly believe their eyes. There is the pair of shoes! Where did they come from? They discuss the mystery. There is a knock at the door. A customer comes in. The customer takes one look at the shoes, and likes them so well he buys them at once. The shoemaker and his wife can hardly believe their good fortune. That night, the shoemaker shows his wife a piece of leather he has bought with the money from the customer. This will be enough for more than one pair of shoes. The shoemaker's wife persuades him to leave the leather until the next day. The two go off to bed.

Once again, the elves arrive. They see the leather. Again, they decide to help. Quickly they set to work and make more shoes. Then, they dance off into the night.

The next morning, when the shoemaker and his wife come in, they are more surprised than before. Again they discuss the mystery. Who has made the shoes? How can they find out? The wife has an idea. Instead of going to bed, they will stay up all night and watch from a hiding place. They will find out who their good friends are.

That night, the shoemaker has an even bigger piece of leather. He leaves it on his workbench. But instead of going off to bed, he and his wife hide behind a screen to see what will happen.

Once again, the elves arrive. They talk about what good people the shoemaker and his wife are. They talk about how they want to help them. And they set to work making more shoes. But this time, the shoemaker and his wife hear every word.

When the elves have finished their work and have gone, the shoemaker and his wife come out from behind the screen. They talk about their good fortune, and decide they must repay the elves. They decide to make each elf a new suit of clothes. How pleased they are at the surprise they are planning for the elves!

The next night, the shoemaker and his wife hide behind the screen once more. Again the elves come dancing in. They go to the work bench to find the leather — but there is no leather. Instead, they find the suits of clothes the shoemaker and his wife have made for them. Each elf is proud of his suit, and tells the others what he likes best about it. Quickly, the elves put on their new clothes and start to dance about.

While they are dancing, the shoemaker and his wife come out of hiding. The elves are caught! The shoemaker and his wife thank them for all their help. The elves thank the shoemaker and his wife for their beautiful new clothes. Then, as it is almost morning, the elves go dancing off, as the shoemaker and his wife wave a happy goodbye.

Columbus and the Queen

The scene is the Court of Spain in the late 15th century. King Ferdinand and Queen Isabella are seated on their thrones. A page announces that Christopher Columbus, an Italian seaman, wishes to see them. The King and Queen say Columbus may enter.

Columbus comes in and bows low. The King asks why Columbus has come to the Court of Spain.

Columbus explains that he is looking for someone to give him the money he needs to make an important journey. He believes that the world is round, not flat. And he believes that he can reach the Indies by sailing west.

The King makes fun of Columbus. Everyone knows the world is flat! If Columbus sails west, he will fall off the edge and be lost.

Columbus shows, using an egg, how the world may, indeed, be a sphere. *(You decide how he does this.)* Queen Isabella is interested. She is impressed by Columbus, and by what he says. She points out to Ferdinand that if Spain gives Columbus the money he needs, Spain will gain great riches when he returns from his voyage.

But Ferdinand will not agree. He claims the voyages will cost too much money, and Columbus will simply disappear. He says nobody should believe the wild dreams of Columbus.

But Isabella believes. And since the King will not give Columbus the money, she decides to give it to him herself. To everyone's amazement, she takes off her crown and all her jewels and gives them to Christopher Columbus. She wishes him success on his journeys.

He, in turn, bows low before her. He thanks her for her kindness and generosity. And he tells her that the whole world will forever remember how good Queen Isabella was to the navigator, Christopher Columbus.

Making Up a Whole Play
of Your Own

Now that you've put on *The Elves and the Shoemaker* and *Columbus and the Queen*, you will probably want to put on more plays. You can make them up yourself! A play is just pantomime and dialogue put together. Since you have already had practice at making up pantomime and dialogue, why not make up a play of your own?

There are many ways to get ideas for the subject of your play. You may use a story that you know. Or perhaps you will choose something that happened in history, such as the *Mayflower* and the landing of the Pilgrims at Plymouth Rock. Some jokes can be turned into short plays. So can some songs — *Rudolf the Red-Nosed Reindeer* and *There Was an Old Woman Who Swallowed a Fly*, for example. Or you can make up your own story.

If you decide to make up your own story, here is a tip to keep in mind: the most interesting plays are based on a problem that must be solved or a question that must be answered. Here are some of the problems and questions that make good plays:

— What is behind a closed door?
— What does the message in code mean?
— Who did it?
— How can the villain be outsmarted?
— Where is the missing clue?
— Where is that weird sound coming from?
— What is that funny smell?

And the most important question of all — the one you want the audience to ask all during your play — is "What happens next?"

3. Acting for Invisible Actors

Have you ever played a joke on someone by hiding? Maybe you hid behind a tree, or perhaps you hid in a closet, or behind the sofa. You probably made funny noises like "Ooooohh" to frighten the person who couldn't see you. He could hear the noise, but he couldn't see where it was coming from. You were invisible.

When you put on a puppet show, the audience can hear your voice. But they can't see you. They can only see the puppets. That's one way you can be an invisible actor.

For a costume party, you put on a mask so nobody can recognize you. Your friends can see you, but they can't see your face. They can hear what you say, but they can't see your expressions as you speak. That's a way of being invisible.

You can put on plays with all the actors wearing masks. Just as at the costume party, people will see you, but they won't see your face. They'll hear you, but they won't see your expressions. That's another way of being an invisible actor.

Have you ever wished you could be truly invisible? That you could be in a room with nobody seeing you? That you could speak so that people would hear you, but they wouldn't be able to see you?

It would take magic to make that wish come true. But if you own a tape recorder, or can borrow one, you can do something like that. You can read a play into the tape recorder. Later, you can play it back for other people to hear. Your voice will come out of the tape recorder, but you won't be moving your lips. You'll be listening to your own voice, just like everyone else. Other people could even listen to the tape when you weren't there. You could be a hundred miles away, but there would be your voice, speaking loud and clear. So that's another way of being an invisible actor.

Begin being invisible actors by using puppets. Then, if you like, you can try the other kinds of invisible acting, too.

Puppets

A puppet is a doll with a hollow body and an opening in the back or the bottom. You slip your hand into the puppet's body. You put your index finger into the puppet's head. You use your fingers to make the puppet move. If you crouch down behind a table or a sofa, and hold the puppet above the edge, the audience can see the puppet without seeing you. When you move your hand, the puppet moves. When you speak, it is as though the puppet were speaking.

You can buy puppets ready-made at some toy shops. But it's much more fun to make your own. And it's not hard to do.

Here are some ideas for very simple puppets you can make easily and quickly:

■ Take a raw potato. Using a vegetable corer, very carefully cut a hole about halfway into the potato, beginning at the smaller end. That is the puppet's head. Test the hole in the head on your index finger or second finger, to make sure it is deep enough for your finger to fit snugly.

Now, make a face on the puppet head. You can do this with felt-tipped markers, or with crayons. Or you can glue pieces of paper on for the face. You can push in two cloves for the eyes. What else would make good eyes? You can glue on some scraps of yarn for hair, if you like. Or you can push toothpicks into the puppet's head for a crown. Also you can punch your finger through the middle of a sheet of plain white paper, to make a covering skirt under the potato head.

What other things could you do to help decorate your puppet? (Remember, though, that puppets made of potatoes don't last very long. So don't spend too much time and effort on them.)

■ Another good puppet head can be made from an old rubber ball. Cut a hole in the ball, big enough for your index finger. Again, the vegetable corer, used very carefully, is a good tool. What kinds of material would be good for decorating a rubber ball to look like a puppet's face?

■ An interesting puppet can be made from an old scrap of thin, smooth cloth. A piece about the size of a man's handkerchief is good. Make a fist, and drop the cloth over it, so that it hangs down around your wrist in points. Now, with a felt-tipped pen, draw a simple face — just eyes, nose, and mouth — on the front of the cloth. See what happens to the puppet's face as you very slowly unclench your fist a tiny bit, then clench it again. Does it make the puppet's face move?

■ For a puppet's body, you can use an old sock or an old mitten. Make a fist, but leave your index finger pointing up. Slip the sock or mitten over your hand, and slide the puppet head down on your index finger. (If the body material is thick, you may find it simpler to cut a small hole in the end for your finger to stick through. Then put the puppet head over your bare finger.)

67

■ Even simpler, put a ready-made puppet head on your finger. Then ask someone to tie a handkerchief or small scarf around your finger, just under the puppet head. You can then arrange the cloth to fall over the rest of your hand, like a flowing robe.

■ The simplest puppets of all — and maybe the funniest — are made of old gloves. Just pull on an old glove, and pretend it's a puppet. That's all there is to it. Hold the glove puppet up where everyone can see it. Announce, "Ladies and gentlemen, I would like you to meet my puppet." If you like, you can tell the puppet's name, and what kind of person he is. "My puppet is a king, named Henry." "My puppet is a dragon, named Snap." Do you know what will happen? Though the puppet may *look* like a glove, everyone in the audience will believe right away that it really *is* a king, or a dragon, or whatever you say it is.

So you see, you really don't need fancy puppets in order to put on a puppet show. Of course, you *can* make puppets that are much fancier than the ones described here if you want to. They take time and effort, but many boys and girls enjoy making them. If you'd like to try, you can surely find a book in the library that will help you.*

Puppet Actions

No matter what kind of puppet you are using — the kind you make yourself or the kind that comes from the store — the most important thing about a puppet show is what the puppets *do*.

Puppets can do almost anything.

---

*One book is *Puppet-Making* by Chester Jay Alkema (1971).

Here are some things puppets can do. Before you put the puppets on your hands, you might like to try practicing some of these moves with your bare hands.

- A puppet can walk very slowly and grandly, like a king in a parade.
- A puppet can walk in short, jerky steps, like a little old lady.
- A puppet can take great leaping hops, like a kangaroo.
- A puppet can glide about, like a boy when he's ice-skating.
- A puppet can jog along like a rider, if he has a puppet horse to ride.
- A puppet can sway back and forth from side to side, like a clock pendulum.
- A puppet can bow forward, very low.
- Two puppets can dance together — side by side, or face to face.
- A puppet can fall flat on his face!

Think of all the things a puppet can do when he's made out of just a glove. All five fingers in the puppet can move. Try using your hand as though it were a glove puppet. Here are some things you can do.

- You can clench and unclench your fist, very quickly.
- You can make your hand into a fist, and then let the fingers uncurl very slowly, like a flower opening its petals.
- One hand can be a fist, and go slamming into the palm of the other hand, which stands open.
- Your two hands can have a fight with one another! Which hand will win — the left or the right?
- Your two hands can move slowly together, until they touch, palm to palm.
- You can wiggle all your fingers very fast — and then, suddenly, stop!

Here is a play you can put on by yourself, with only a glove on each hand. There are two characters in the play, Left and Right. Both characters can be wearing the same kind of glove, or they can be in different gloves. Which would be better? You decide.

Left and Right

At the start of the play, Left is all alone. He is standing straight up, palm out, fingers together. Slowly, as though he were yawning, he stretches out his fingers. He gives them a good shaking. Then he stands still again.

Now, Right comes along. He is in a loose fist, and is walking along minding his own business. How do you suppose Right might walk?

Then, Right sees Left. He stops. Left doesn't see Right — or if he does, he ignores him.

Right tries to attract Left's attention. How could he do that? He might jump up and down a few times. He might waggle his fingers. He might knock his fist on a table to make some noise. Or he might do something else. You decide, then act it out.

But Left still pays no attention. So Right goes up to Left and with his index finger, taps him on the shoulder.

Left, startled, slides away from Right and turns to face him.

Right bows low, as though saying, "How do you do?"

But Left is a rude fellow. He turns his back on Right.

Right steps back a bit to think things over. Then, he curls into a very tight fist, sails over to Left, and knocks him over. He then steps back to see what Left will do.

Very slowly, Left picks himself up. He gives two little shakes, to get the dust off himself. Slowly, he turns to face Right, and begins moving toward him, like an angry king. Now Right becomes a little frightened. He trembles.

Suddenly, Left attacks! Slap, slap! So Right fights back. Wham! Bam! How do you suppose the two hands would fight

one another? Would they give slaps back and forth? Perhaps they might get into a clinch, with both hands clasped, and twist back and forth a few times. Would they collide head on, fist against fist? Or bump each other side by side, thumb against thumb? You decide.

Finally, both hands are worn out. They are lying in a heap, panting for breath. First one, then the other, pulls himself upright and shakes himself off. Both are panting a bit for breath. (You can pant for the puppets.)

They turn to face each other — and decide to be friends. So they shake hands. How would hands shake hands? Would the two hands fold together slowly? Would Left touch his thumb to Right's little finger?

After they've shaken hands, the two go off together as friends. Would they link thumbs? Or would Right clasp Left? You decide — then, act it out!

Here are some rhymes that are fun to act out with glove puppets.

Finger Game Rhymes

Here's my thumb — that's for a ladybug.
Pointing finger — that's for a beetle.
Hi, diddle, diddle — what's in the middle?
Green grasshopper with his hind-leg fiddle.
Ring finger, ring finger — that's for a bee.
Finger on the end? Why, that's for a flea!

How would you like a little red hen?
Here's how to catch one before I count ten.
> Make a fist,
> Flick your wrist,
> Give it a shake,
> And give it a twist.

Say the secret message,
"Tiggle, tiggle, tout,"
Then open your fist
So the hen can get out.

Didn't you see the little red hen?
Well, all I can say is — try it again!
The thumb is a dwarf on the side of a hill.
The pointer is a giant, silent and still.
The middle finger's the horse they ride.
The fourth is the sword they keep by their side.
The fifth is a watchman who stands through the night,
And gives them the signal when trouble's in sight.
When he shouts out his warning that trouble is near,
They quickly make a fist — and all disappear!

Here is another play for two glove puppets. In this play, the characters speak. If you are putting on the play by yourself, taking both parts, you may want to use two different voices. One voice could be high and squeaky, and one voice could be low and growly. Or one voice could be your own voice, while the other voice could be a funny voice. You decide.

The Handsomest Hand

Left (excitedly): Right! Right! Have you heard the news?

Right: The news? What news?

Left: The King has announced a contest. They're giving a prize for the handsomest hand in all the land.

Right: The handsomest hand in all the land? Why, I'll bet I win!

Left: You? Don't make me laugh. I am the handsomest hand in all the land, and I bet I win that prize — easy as snapping my fingers. *(He snaps his fingers.)*

Right: How can you be the handsomest hand? I'm taller than you are. See? *(He stretches himself up to his full height.)*

Left (also stretching himself): I'm just as tall as you are — if not taller.

Right: But look how wide I can stretch my fingers.

Left: Look how wide I can stretch *my* fingers.

Right: But your fingers aren't as talented as mine are, Left. I'll bet you can't do this! *(What does Right do with his fingers?)*

Left: Yes, I can. See? *(He imitates Right.)*

Right: Well, then, how about this? *(What does he do?)*

Left: That's easy. *(He imitates Right.)* But I'll bet you can't do this! *(What does he do?)*

Right: Look, I'll prove to you *I* am the handsomest hand in all the land. I'll do my very best trick. *(What is it?)*

Left: Why, that's *my* very best trick. And I do it just as well as you. See? *(He does the same trick.)*

Right: I think you're right, Left. You and I are evenly matched. I'd say our talents go hand in hand.

Left: I have an idea! Why don't we *both* enter the contest. I'll bet together we're the handsomest *pair* of hands in all the land.

Right: Oh, that's a wonderful idea! You know something, Left? I really have to hand it to you!

You can make up lots of plays for glove puppets. Some you can do by yourself. Others can be done by two or more people wearing glove puppets. Here are some ideas to get you started.

■ A parade of dinosaurs.

■ A game of catch, using an imaginary ball.

■ A contest between a group of gloves and a group of mittens to see who can make the best snowballs.

■ A play telling what happened to the six little mittens that were lost by the three little kittens in the nursery rhyme.

Glove puppets are also good dancers. You might like to put some music on the record player, and then let your hands dance to it. They would sway lazily during the slow parts of the music, and move more quickly during the fast parts. What would the fingers do when the music got very loud? What would they do when the music got soft? See how many different movements you can make with your hands to help express the music that is playing.

If you are using regular puppets — the kinds with heads and faces — you can put on regular plays with them. Since puppets can do almost anything real people can do, you can use the same kinds of plays for puppets that you use when you are being actors yourselves.

Some of the plays you have already read in this book would make wonderful plays for puppets. Why not act one of them out? It would be especially interesting to do *Pippy and Diddy Get a Surprise* and *The Mysterious Something* as puppet plays. What kind of a puppet will the Mysterious Something turn out to be?

Masks

When you act, you are pretending to be somebody different from the person you really are. Sometimes that can be hard. Sometimes you don't feel the things the character should feel. So how can you show them? For example, imagine that a character is supposed to get very, very angry. He is supposed to yell. He is supposed to say hateful things. Now, imagine that the actor who is playing the part of the angry person is a very shy, quiet boy. He may not like to feel angry. He may not like to yell. He may not like to say hateful things. What can he do?

He can put on a mask. When an actor wears a mask, it is often easier for him to say and do things he wouldn't really do as himself. The shy boy who doesn't like to shout may find that he is able to shout if he has on a mask.

And when the actor wears a mask, it helps the audience, too. The mask reminds the audience that it isn't really the shy boy who is making all that noise. It is the character the shy boy is playing.

The usefulness of masks has been known for thousands of years. As far back as history goes, men were using masks to help them be better actors. Many of the masks had the faces of gods on them. Actors wanted to have the gods take part in their plays. But the actors were men. How could they pretend to be gods? They decided it would be easier to pretend to be a god if they wore the mask of a god. You may be able to find pictures of these masks if you look in an encyclopedia in the school library under "Masks."

What kinds of masks can you use? Any kind you like! If you have a mask left over from a costume party, you can wear it. It doesn't matter whether it is the kind that covers your whole face or the kind that covers just your eyes.

Making Masks

Or you can make a mask for yourself. Here's how.

Get a big paper bag — one that is big enough to go down over your head easily without being torn.

Slip the bag over your head until it rests on your shoulders. Then, carefully mark on the front of the bag the places where your eyes and nose are. Someone can do this for you, or you can do it yourself. Either pinch the paper, to make a crease in it, or find the right spots with the fingers of one hand and then mark them gently with a felt-tipped pen held in your other hand.

When you have marked the eye and nose places, take the bag off. Using scissors, carefully cut out holes at the spots you have marked. You may have to try putting the mask on several times to be sure the holes are in the right places and that they are big enough for you to see through.

When you have the holes cut in the right places, you are ready to decorate your mask. You can do this with just about any art supplies you happen to have. Felt-tipped marking pens, crayons, and poster paints are all good. So are artist's pencils and water paints.*

If you want, you can glue things on to your mask, too. Here are some ideas of things to glue on your mask:

- Scraps of ribbon, yarn, or cloth trimmings.
- Pieces of bright construction paper or aluminum foil.
- Pieces of uncooked macaroni in interesting shapes and designs.
- Feathers or dried leaves.
- Scraps of gift wrapping paper or illustrations from old magazines.
- Paper clips, or toothpicks, or sequins.

What other things can you think of that you could use to help decorate your mask? Use your imagination. The wilder your mask is, the better!

And what kind of face will you put on your mask? Will it be a clown? A beautiful lady? A lion? A polar bear? Perhaps you will want it to be a monster of some kind, or a creature from outer space.

If you find pictures of masks, you can copy those if you like. But usually it's more fun to follow your own idea. That way, you'll be sure that nobody else in the world will have a mask that looks quite like yours.

* You can make masks out of cardboard or corrugated cartons, too. See the book *Masks* by Chester Jay Alkema (1971).

Once you have made your mask, what kind of play will you use it for? You can use any of the plays you have already read, of course. For instance, you could put on *Hansel and Gretel,* which appears in the section on Pantomime, with all of the actors wearing masks. Think of what a good mask you could make for the witch! Should the person who reads the story aloud wear a mask?

Or you could make masks for the Shoemaker and his wife and for all the elves. What kind of faces would elves have? Green? Violet? Yellow? All different shades? And think of the fun you could have making the animal masks for the play, *The Mysterious Something.*

There's one special kind of play that you can use masks for, though, that is particularly good. It's a play in which there is a problem, and the actors have to work out the problem together. You've already had some practice at figuring out how to make up the end of a play. You did it in *Mr. Higglebee's Robots* and you did it in *The Escape of the Monkeys.* Even though each of these new mask plays is about a problem, it shouldn't be a problem for you!

A Problem for the Animals

(The scene is a barnyard. A Cow, a Cat, a Dog, and a Robin are there. Suddenly a loud squawking noise is heard, and Mrs. Hen comes rushing in.)

Mrs. Hen: Kut, kut, k-daw-kut! Kut, kut, k-daw-kut! Help! Help!

Cow: Moo. What's all this noise about, Mrs. Hen?

Cat: Meow. What's the trouble?

Dog: Woof, woof. Why all the noise?

Robin: Tweet, tweet. Is someone in trouble?

Mrs. Hen: Kut, kut, k-daw-kut! The most terrible thing has happened.

Other Animals: Tell us!

Mrs. Hen: One of my chicks has disappeared. He's gone! My little Elmer is missing from the nest!

Cow: Have you looked all over the hen-house for him?

Cat: Have you looked all over the barnyard for him?

Dog: Have you looked in the stables and down by the brook?

Mrs. Hen: Yes, I've looked everywhere, and I can't find him.

Robin: But he must be somewhere.

Mrs. Hen: He isn't anywhere. Do you know what I think? I think the Fox came and carried him away.

Cow: That's a serious thing to say, Mrs. Hen. Are you sure it was the Fox?

Mrs. Hen: What other explanation could there be?

Cat: I don't think it was the Fox. I haven't seen him for a week.

Dog: I don't think it was the Fox. Don't you remember he promised to be good?

Cow: I don't think it was the Fox. I think you just haven't looked hard enough.

Robin: I don't think it was the Fox. Elmer is too smart to let the Fox get him.

Mrs. Hen: I thought you were my friends! But you're no help at all. I say it must have been the Fox, and you say it couldn't have been. If you were my friends, you'd help me find Elmer. If you were my friends, you'd help me catch the fox!

Robin: We *are* your friends, Mrs. Hen. And we *will* help you.

Mrs. Hen: How? How will you help me?

What happens next? Mrs. Hen has a problem. Her chick is missing. But the other animals have a problem, too. They don't think Mrs. Hen is being fair to the Fox. They have their own ideas about how they can help best.

How will the animals solve the problem? They will have to talk over the matter, looking at it from all sides, before they can decide.

Will the animals help Mrs. Hen? There's only one way to find out. Act it out — and see what happens!

Here is another problem for you to solve. This time, it's a problem for a boy and his sister, rather than for animals. So put on your masks, and see if you can help this family solve their problem.

A Problem for Joe and Janice

(The scene is a living room. The people there are Father, Mother, Joe, and Janice.)

Father: Tomorrow is Sunday, and the weather man says it is going to be a nice day. What shall we do?

Mother: I think it would be fun to go for a drive somewhere.

Joe: I know! Let's go to the park. We can see the animals at the zoo, and then play in the playground.

Janice: No, I don't want to go to the park. I want to visit Grandma instead. Wouldn't you rather do that, Mother?

Mother: They both sound like good ideas. I think you children should decide.

Joe: Dad said the weather is going to be nice. That makes it perfect to go to the park. We can visit Grandma some time when it's raining.

Janice: But the things at the park are mostly fun for boys. I don't enjoy the playground as much as you do, Joe. And I think we should do something we all enjoy.

Joe: Oh, you never want me to have any fun. You're always thinking of yourself!

Janice: That's not so. Besides, we always do what you want to do. I think it's my turn to choose.

Joe: We went to the circus, didn't we? You wanted to go to the circus.

Janice: Yes, but so did you. And didn't Dad take you to the football game, because that's what you wanted? I had to stay home.

Mother: You could have gone to the football game if you'd wanted to, Janice.

Father: If you children can't agree, we won't do anything at all tomorrow. We'll just stay home.

Joe: Oh, Dad, could we do both? Go to the park first, and then go on to Grandma's house?

Father: No, Joe, there won't be time to do both. One or the other. Now make up your minds.

Joe and Janice are becoming angry with each other. What will they say to each other? What will Mother say? What will Father say? How will the problem be solved? Act it out!

If you are acting out this mask play in school, there may be children in the audience who have a different idea about how the problem could be solved. So after one group has acted the play out to the end, you might want to have the play all over again with a new group of children. With different actors and different masks, it will be almost a completely different play!

Here is another story about children with a problem. This time, though, the actors have to make up all the words. If you acted out *Columbus and the Queen* at the end of the last chapter, you've already had practice at this sort of thing.

A Problem for Barbara

Barbara is a new girl in school. She doesn't have any friends. Tim feels sorry for Barbara, and so does Tim's sister, Carol. After school, they meet in the schoolyard and decide to be friends with Barbara.

But Carol's best friend, Miriam, wants to walk home with Carol. And Miriam doesn't like Barbara. Which girl will Carol choose?

Two boys in Tim's class, Randy and Nick, have invited him to come and play ball with them. It's the first time they've asked him to play, and Tim is afraid that if he says "No," they may not ask him again. What does Tim decide to do?

To solve this problem, choose three girls (one to be Barbara, one to be Carol, and one to be Miriam) and three boys (one to be Tim, one to be Randy, and one to be Nick). Then, put on your masks — and act it out!

Of course, you don't *always* have to wear masks when you make up plays about problems. But if it helps you to be more comfortable, then wear the mask. Besides, these plays are usually more fun to watch when everyone is wearing a mask he made himself.

Recording a Play

If you have a tape recorder, or there is one you can use, you might like to make a tape recording of a play. In a tape recorder play, the whole story must be told in words, as there is no way to see what the people in the story are doing. But the actors don't have to memorize the words. They can read them into the microphone — or they can make them up as they go along.

An important part of a tape recorder play is sound effects. These are special noises that are planned to be included in the play. Here are some of the sound effects that there might be in a tape recorder play. If you heard these sounds, what would you think they were telling you?

— A door slamming shut.
— The rattle of knives and forks against a plate.
— A sharp slap.
— A big splash.
— A piece of paper being rattled.

Making Sound Effects

Using sound effects is a good way to help make your tape recorder play sound as though the story is really happening. You have to use your imagination in making the sounds. You may want to practice two or three different ways to make a sound until you get the one that is best. Here are some suggestions of some of the sounds you can make — and how to make them.

■ For a horse galloping, sit in a chair with your knees together. Holding your hands just a few inches above your thighs, slap your right hand against your left hand. Without stopping, move your right hand down to slap your right thigh. Then slap your left hand against your left thigh. Repeat it several times, quickly. It takes practice — but you will find it really does sound like horses' hoofs.

■ For a fire, crinkle a piece of cellophane next to the microphone. Stiff cellophane — the kind that comes wrapped around some packages — works best. The filmy kind that clings doesn't have enough "crackle" to it.

■ For rain falling, try putting a cupful of dry, uncooked rice in the bottom of a small box. Shake the box gently so that the rice moves about. This takes practice, too, to make it sound just right.

■ For wind howling, make a sort of whistling noise into the microphone — but without really whistling. Pucker up as though you really were going to whistle. Then, let the air escape through your mouth with less speed and force than it would take to whistle.

Keep practicing these sounds. Very quickly you'll be an expert at making them!

What other kinds of sounds do you want to make? And how would you make them? It can be a lot of fun just trying out different noises to see how they come out on the tape recorder.

Here is a play written especially to be acted for the tape recorder. Note that one of the characters is called "Narrator." A *narrator* is one who tells a story. The Narrator in this play is very much like the Reader you needed to put on *Hansel and Gretel* and *Pippy and Diddy Get a Surprise*.

Clang, the Clumsy Elf

Sound: Wind whistling fiercely.

Narrator: Have you ever heard the story of Clang, the Clumsy Elf? He worked in Santa's Workshop, at the North Pole. He was a kind-hearted elf, and really tried to help Santa Claus in the important work of getting ready for Christmas. But no matter what he tried to do, Clang always seemed to get into trouble.

Sound: Wind stops.

Clang: What are you doing, Merrylog?

Merrylog: I'm painting these rocking-horses.

Clang: May I help you?

Merrylog: I'd be happy to have some help, Clang. There are only a few nights left before Christmas, and I have a great many horses still to paint.

Clang: What shall I do to help?

Merrylog: Just get a brush and a can of paint from the shelf, and begin to work on those horses over there.

Clang: Oh dear! The shelf is so high. The only way I can reach the paint is to stand on tip-toe. Let — me — try. Oh!

Sound: Loud bonk of can falling off shelf, splash of paint.

Narrator: Splash! Clang had knocked the can of paint off the shelf. The paint went flying everywhere, and covered poor Clang from head to foot.

Merrylog (angrily): Now look at the mess you've made. You'd better go and clean yourself up, Clang. And in the future don't come messing around my paint shop. You're too clumsy.

Narrator: Poor Clang. He was only trying to help. It wasn't his fault that he was clumsy. Maybe there was something else he could do.

Clang: Hello, Twinkletime! What are you doing?

Twinkletime: Oh, it's you, is it, Clang? I'm packing up the ornaments for the Christmas trees of the world. See the hundreds and hundreds of boxes that have to be filled? Sometimes

I wonder if I'll ever get them all packed in time for Christmas.

Clang: Then maybe you can use my help. I'd be glad to help you, Twinkletime.

Twinkletime: That would be wonderful, Clang. You can begin by taking these boxes that I've already filled with ornaments out to the loading platform. Then they'll be all set to go into Santa's sleigh.

Clang: Glad to help, Twinkletime.

Narrator: So Clang picked up a great big box filled with beautiful glass Christmas ornaments, and began to carry it out of the workshop. But the box was so big, Clang couldn't see where he was going. And suddenly —

Sound: Crash of box falling and glass ornaments breaking.

Narrator: Crash! Clang had slipped, and all the beautiful glass Christmas ornaments lay broken in a million pieces, all over the floor.

Twinkletime (angrily): Is that what you call help, Clang? Breaking all my ornaments?

Clang (sadly): I can't help it, Twinkletime. I'm truly sorry. It's just that I'm so clumsy.

Twinkletime: I know it's not your fault, Clang. But in the future, you'd better find some other work to do. Something that's not so breakable.

Narrator: Poor Clang. He only wanted to help — but everywhere he went, it was the same story.

Sound: Splash.

An Elf: Oh, Clang! You've tipped over a whole pot of cookie batter!

Sound: Wood splintering.

87

Another Elf: Oh, Clang! You've broken that nice new sled I was making.

Sound: A great clattering noise.

Yet Another Elf: Oh, Clang! Look what you've done! You've knocked a whole carton of blocks down the stairs!

Narrator: Clang was so unhappy. He only wanted to help, but he couldn't seem to do anything right. At last, he couldn't think of another thing to do.

Clang: Everywhere I go, I run into the same problem. Too clumsy to be of any help. I'll just have to go away and leave this Workshop. There's no place for me here.

Narrator: So little Clang, the clumsy elf, packed his few belongings in a suitcase, and made ready to leave the North Pole Workshop. He shook hands with all the other elves, and said goodbye. He went out to the barn, and said a special goodbye to all the reindeer. Finally, there was just one last person left for Clang to say goodbye to.

Sound: Knock on door.

Santa Claus (from a short distance): Come in.

Sound: Door opening and closing.

Santa Claus: Why, Clang! How are you, my little elf friend? But — what's this? You're carrying a suitcase.

Clang: That's right, Santa Claus. I've come to say goodbye. I'm leaving the North Pole forever.

Santa Claus: Leaving the North Pole, Clang? Why?

Clang: I can't seem to do anything right, Santa Claus. I spilled a whole can of paint, and I broke a whole carton of Christmas ornaments. I overturned a pot of cookie batter, and I broke one of the new Christmas sleds. I even dropped a whole

box of building blocks down the Workshop stairs. I'm just too clumsy to be any use, Santa Claus, and so I've decided to leave.

Santa Claus: Hmm. This is a serious problem, Clang. I'm sure there's work here that you could do, and I'd hate to lose such a good elf as you. Besides, the only reason you're clumsy is that you're growing. Why, one year from now, you'll be all over your clumsiness.

Clang: I — I will?

Santa Claus: To be sure, you will. So the question is, what can you do in the meantime?

Clang: There's nothing I can do. Everywhere I go I just break things, or drop things, or spill things, or stumble over things. I just keep making one mess after another.

Santa Claus (happily): That gives me the perfect idea! Clang, if you're so good at making a mess, I'll bet you'd be extra good at cleaning them up. How would you like to be Chief Custodian of Santa's Workshop?

Clang (happily): Do you really mean it, Santa Claus?

Santa Claus: I do indeed! From now on, you'll be in charge of all the mops and brooms and dustpans. And when a mess is made, it won't be Clang who made it. It will be Clang who cleans it up. We've needed someone around here for a long time who can keep things ship-shape and tidy, and you're the perfect elf for the job.

Clang (happily): Oh, thank you, Santa Claus. If I can do that, I won't care if people call me Clang the Clumsy Elf.

Santa Claus: But they won't call you that any more. From now on, you'll be Clang, the Custodian Elf. You'll be Clang, the Custodian of Christmas!

Here is another play for you to act for the tape recorder. Unlike *Clang, the Clumsy Elf*, which was a story of make-believe, this play tells a bit about some important women in history. Perhaps you will want to find out more about these women. Your teacher or librarian will be able to help you.

They Were Brave

Narrator: Have you ever found yourself day-dreaming in class? You know you should be listening to the teacher. But somehow, your mind just wanders off by itself. This is the story of a girl named Carol, and of the wonderful day-dream she had one day at school.

Sound: Ruler being rapped on a desk to command attention.

Teacher: Now, class, we are going to talk about great heroes of history. Who remembers what I asked you to think about last night?

Joe: You asked us to think about the brave men of the past.

Teacher: Right. And I asked you to be prepared to tell me who you think was the bravest man of all time. Joe, can you suggest someone?

Joe: I think Abraham Lincoln was a very brave man.

Harry: What about Christopher Columbus?

Nick: I think Martin Luther King, Jr., was an especially brave man.

Teacher: Those are good ideas. What other suggestions are there for brave men?

Various Voices: General Eisenhower ... Winston Churchill ... John Glenn ... Sitting Bull ...

Teacher: Carol, what about you? *(Short pause.)* Carol!

Carol (as though surprised): What? Oh, I'm sorry, Miss Grant. I'm afraid I wasn't listening.

Teacher: I asked you what name you wish to suggest for our list of brave men.

Carol: I — I don't know about brave *men*, Miss Grant. I suppose I was thinking about brave women.

Joe (laughing): Women! That's silly.

Nick: Everyone knows men are braver than women.

Harry: Oh, Carol, you really aren't thinking today.

Teacher: That's enough, boys. Carol, have you a name of a brave man to offer for our list?

Carol: I — I don't think so, Miss Grant.

Teacher (sternly): I'm very disappointed in you, Carol.

Carol (sadly): Yes, Miss Grant.

Teacher: Now, class, back to our list.

Narrator: Poor Carol! She had tried to think of a really brave man. But no matter how hard she tried, she found her mind kept wandering. She found herself thinking of women instead — women she had heard about, or read about. And if she closed her eyes, it almost seemed as though Carol could actually see those women, and hear them speak.

Sound: Wind.

Joan (softly): Carol . . . Carol . . .

Carol: Why — who are you?

Joan: I am a woman from the past, Carol. I've come to tell you I think you were right. Women *can* be brave.

Carol (doubtfully) : None of the other kids think so. They say only men face the real tests of courage.

Joan (laughing softly) : Ah, I've heard *that* story before. When I went to Robert de Baudricourt and asked for a horse and suit of armour, he laughed because I was a woman. When I went to the Dauphin of France, and promised not only to crown him King but also to drive the English from our land, he laughed, too, because I was a woman. But I was right, and those who laughed were wrong.

Carol (wonderingly) : I know who you are! You're Joan of Arc.

Joan: Did it not take courage to lead an army of poor, frightened soldiers against the mighty and successful English? Did it not take courage to stand the jeers and insults and tortures when I was imprisoned?

Carol: Oh, Joan, you *were* brave. Bravest of all when you met your death.

Joan: Do not forget, Carol, that women can be as brave as men, as long as they are fighting for what is right.

Carol: I won't forget, I won't. Wait till I remind the boys in class about you. They think only a man can be a soldier. But Joan of Arc was as brave a soldier as ever lived.

Harriet: Is that what bravery means, Carol? Being a soldier?

Carol: Who — who are you?

Harriet: I wasn't a soldier, although I faced death many and many a time in the days before and during America's Civil War.

Carol: How? Where?

Harriet: Have you ever heard of the Underground Slave Railway? I was one of those who spent a lifetime bringing men and women out of slavery, and smuggling them North, where they could be free.

Carol: Now I know you. You're Harriet Tubman.

Harriet: Yes, child, that is my name.

Carol: I've read about you. You were the most important person on the whole Underground Railway. Southern slave-owners once offered a huge reward if you could be captured — but that didn't stop you. Because of your efforts, thousands of slaves found their way to freedom.

Harriet: My work was different from Joan of Arc's work — but don't you think it took courage for a black woman in those days to do what I did?

Carol: You bet I do! Just wait till I tell the boys about you.

Florence: And will you tell the boys about me, too, Carol?

Carol: You? It's hard to believe that such a beautiful and finely dressed lady as you could have been a brave heroine.

Florence (laughing lightly): Oh, I don't claim any credit for myself. That really wouldn't be ladylike, and I was brought up always to· do the right thing. Please don't misunderstand. It's just that I think your friends should be reminded of how hard it can be, sometimes, for a woman to be allowed to do even the simplest thing — like being a nurse.

Carol: Is that what you wanted to be? A nurse?

Florence: More than anything else in the world. But in my day, it was thought unfit work for a lady. Perhaps you won't believe how hard I had to fight, how many things I had to overcome, before I was allowed to go into the fields during the Crimean War to set up the first really clean, well-run battle-field hospitals.

Carol: Then you must be Florence Nightingale — "The Lady of the Lamp."

Florence: Yes, Carol, that is who I am. Oh, I admit that next to women like Joan of Arc and Harriet Tubman, what I've done must seem very small.

Carol: Not at all! In your way you were brave — very brave. Because of what you did, nursing became a highly respected profession, and wounded soldiers are now given the best medical attention possible instead of being treated like mere cattle as they once were.

Florence: It seems simple, now. But I often think how hard a fight it was to win that small victory!

Clara: Florence Nightingale is right, Carol. My battles were like hers — a seemingly endless round of fighting with men who wouldn't listen, just because I was a woman. But if I had given up, today there might be no International Red Cross.

Carol: The Red Cross? Then you must be Clara Barton.

Clara: That is indeed who I am.

Carol: Oh, I've read about you in school. You *were* brave, Mrs. Barton. You may not have had a military enemy to fight, but your battles were as noble in their own way. You are one of the truly brave women.

Anne: Is there room in your list, I wonder, Carol, for one who was only a girl like yourself? I should like you to tell your classmates a little bit about me.

Carol: You *are* only a girl. What battles did you fight?

Anne (shyly): In a way, I didn't fight any battles at all. In fact, I went into hiding — and that's the opposite of fighting. My family were Jews in Holland during World War II, and to save our lives, we lived hidden in an attic for four years.

Finally we were found, however, so we didn't save ourselves after all.

Carol: But you never lost your will to go on living, or your faith in the beauty of life, did you, Anne Frank? In spite of everything that was done to you by your enemies, you could

write, "I still believe that people are basically good at heart."
Oh, that *was* brave!

Anne: Sometimes, I think, it is the battles we fight inside ourselves that take the most courage of all. Look, Carol. There is another woman who fought such a battle.

Carol: I see her. But why doesn't she speak? Why doesn't she seem to see me?

Anne: She cannot speak. She cannot hear. She cannot see. And yet, perhaps, she is one of the bravest women who ever lived. Her name is Helen Keller.

Carol: Helen Keller.

Anne: With the help of a teacher, Helen Keller learned to break out of her world of darkness and silence. Not only did she refuse to be held down by her handicaps, but she became one of the most important and influential women of her time.

Carol: Yes, she was brave. You were *all* brave! I *told* them women could be brave! I told them!

Sound: Wind.

Carol (muttering): I told them! I told them!

Teacher: Carol! What *is* it you're saying?

Carol (happily): Oh, Miss Grant. The boys were wrong. They *were* brave. They were!

Teacher: Who were brave, Carol?

Carol: Joan of Arc and Harriet Tubman. Florence Nightingale and Clara Barton. Anne Frank and Helen Keller.

Teacher: Boys, I think we all owe Carol an apology. The women she has mentioned certainly belong on any list of the world's great heroes. These women had courage to match any man's. Yes, class, Carol is right. They *were* brave.

4. Acting in Chorus

Have you ever heard a choral reading? It's something like a tape recorder play, but not exactly the same.

In a choral reading, small groups of people speak as one person. Each group is called a Chorus. Everyone in the Chorus says the same words at the same time. It takes a lot of practice to be sure that everyone speaks at the same time and pauses at the same time. But it is worth doing. It's great fun — and the effect is very interesting.

One of the things that makes it interesting is that you speak a bit differently in a choral reading from the way you usually do. You say words more slowly. You use more emphasis — that is, you say some words more loudly and clearly than others. You say the words with more rhythm. You use more pauses.

Perhaps that sounds terribly hard. Really, choral readings aren't that difficult. Try them and see!

Here is a choral reading you may like to record on your tape recorder, after you have rehearsed it several times. Or you can put it on just by reading it aloud from your seats in the classroom. Or you can arrange yourselves in groups on a stage. There are a number of different ways in which you can put on a choral reading.

The Emperor's New Clothes

Chorus I: "The Emperor's New Clothes."

Chorus II: A fable . . . by Hans Christian Andersen.

Chorus I: Many years ago there was an Emperor who loved new clothes better than anything else in the world.

Chorus II: He spent all his money on new clothes.

Chorus I: He spent all his time trying on new clothes.

Chorus II: And every closet in his castle was crammed with clothes.

Chorus I: How that Emperor loved clothes!

Chorus II: One day, two men who called themselves weavers came to town.

Chorus I: But they weren't really weavers. Oh, no!

Chorus II: They were rogues. They were rascals.

Chorus I: They were thieves.

Chorus II: One was called Blik and one was called Blan.

Chorus I: And together they thought up a very sly plan.

Blik: I tell you, Blan, I have an idea that will make us both rich.

Blan: That's the kind of scheme I like best. What's your idea, Blik?

Blik: You know how the Emperor loves new clothes.

Blan: Everyone knows that.

Blik: Well, here's what we're going to do. *(Makes whispering sounds.)* Pss-pss-pss-pss-pss.

Blan: That's a wonderful idea, Blik! You're a genius!

Chorus I: What was the scheme? What was the plan?

Chorus II: What could be the plot of Blik and Blan?

Chorus I: The two evil weavers sent a message to the Emperor.

Chorus II: They asked to see him. They said they had something that would make the Emperor very happy.

Sound: Fanfare.

Page (announcing): Your Majesty, here are the weavers, Blik and Blan.

Emperor: You are the two weavers who have something that will make me very happy?

Blik and Blan (together): Yes, Your Majesty.

Emperor: What is it? Tell me!

Blik: We are the most skilled weavers in the world, Your Majesty.

Blan: And what we have is the skill to weave a special kind of cloth — a cloth so special its like has never been seen before.

Emperor: What's so special about this kind of cloth?

Blik: It's magic cloth!

Emperor: Magic?

Blan: Yes!

Blik: It is more beautiful than any other cloth. It is softer than any other cloth. It is more richly decorated than any other cloth.

Blan: But the magic is that it is completely invisible to anyone who is stupid.

Blik: I can see it. Blan can see it. Of course, Your Majesty will be able to see it. But anyone who is *stupid* will *not* be able to see it.

Blan: Would you like a suit of this wonderful cloth, Your Majesty?

Emperor: Yes, yes! I must have you weave me a wonderful suit of clothes.

Blik: Excellent, Your Majesty.

Blan: That will be fifty gold coins, Your Majesty.

Blik (pause): In advance, Your Majesty.

Chorus I: And so the Emperor, who loved clothes more than anything else in the world, ordered a suit to be made by Blik and Blan.

Chorus II: Blik and Blan set up their loom right away.

Chorus I: Busily, they set to work. How their fingers flew!

Chorus II: But they were playing a trick on the Emperor. They were not using real thread. They were not using real cloth. They were only pretending to weave. That was their scheme!

Blik: How clever we are, Blan. Here we sit, moving our fingers back and forth through the air, pretending to weave cloth.

Blan: But nobody will dare say so. They will think they don't see the cloth because they're stupid.

Blik: And nobody will want to admit that he is stupid.

Chorus I: At last the day came when the wonderful suit of clothes was to be ready. The Emperor called one of the most important people of his court, the Chamberlain.

Emperor: Chamberlain, go and fetch the weavers, Blik and Blan. It's time to put on my brand-new suit of clothes.

Chamberlain: Yes, Your Majesty.

Chorus II: So the Chamberlain went to the weavers. But when they held up the clothes, the Chamberlain couldn't see a thing.

Chorus I: The Chamberlain thought to himself . . .

Chamberlain: Oh dear, oh dear. I don't see a thing! It must be that I am stupid. The weavers said that the cloth would be invisible to anyone who was stupid. I'd better *pretend* to see something, so nobody finds out how stupid I am.

Chorus I: And so the Chamberlain said aloud . . .

Chamberlain: Oh, Blik! Oh, Blan! Never in my life have I seen such a beautiful suit of clothes! Come with me to the Emperor.

Chorus II: So the plan was working.

Blik: You see, Blan? He's pretending to see something he doesn't see, because he's afraid to admit he's stupid.

Blan: That only proves how stupid he really is!

Chorus I: Of course, the Emperor didn't see anything either.

Chorus II: There was nothing to be seen.

Chorus I: But the Emperor didn't wish to appear stupid, either. So he said . . .

Emperor: Why, never in my life have I seen such a beautiful suit of clothes!

Blik: We are pleased that you are pleased, Your Majesty.

Blan: Let us help you put on this wonderful suit, Your Majesty. Then everyone can see how marvellous you look.

Chorus I: And so the Emperor put on his new suit of clothes, and went for a walk through his kingdom.

Chorus II: Everywhere he went, the same thing happened.

Chorus I: Nobody could see his clothes. But nobody wanted to be thought stupid. And so everyone said . . .

Group of Men: Now, that's what I call a splendid suit!

Group of Women: It's the most beautiful suit I've ever seen!

Group of Men: So handsome! So rich! So fine!

Group of Women: What a seam! What a stitch! What a line!

Chorus II: And the Emperor said . . .

Emperor: This is the finest suit of clothes I have ever owned. I decree that Blik and Blan are to be given an extra hundred pieces of gold.

Chorus I: And then — a curious thing happened.

Chorus II: A little boy caught sight of the Emperor.

Chorus I: He didn't know anything about the wonderful suit of clothes.

Chorus II: He didn't know what he was supposed to pretend to see.

Chorus I: He only knew what he really did see.

Little Boy: How funny! The Emperor is walking around in his underwear!

Chorus I: At first, everyone was shocked. Everyone gasped in horror.

Chorus II: But then, people suddenly realized a curious something.

Man: This little boy is right!

Group of Women: Ha, ha, ha! The Emperor is walking around in his underwear!

Group of Men: Ho, ho, ho! The Emperor is walking around in his underwear!

Little Boy: Hee, hee, hee! The Emperor is walking around in his underwear!

Chorus I: Soon, the Emperor was the laughing-stock of the kingdom.

Chorus II: Everyone was telling the truth. They couldn't see any clothes.

Chorus I: Everyone, that is, except the Emperor himself.

Chorus II: He was too proud to admit the truth. He was too stubborn to admit the truth.

Emperor (angrily): I *am* wearing a beautiful suit of clothes! I am, I am, I am! The only reason everyone says I'm not is they're all too stupid to see!

Chorus I (sighing): Ah, the poor Emperor. The truth of the matter was . . .

Chorus II: He was the stupidest one of all.

Chorus I: And that is the story of "The Emperor's New Clothes."

Chorus II: By Hans Christian Andersen.

Here is another choral reading play based on an old well-known story. All the words are given for this play, too — but at one point the actors have to sing a song. You'll have to decide what song it will be.

The Bremen Musicians

Chorus I: What happens to an animal that is tired and old?

Chorus II: What happens to a beast who is worn out and no good for service?

Chorus I: Here is a story of four such animals. It is called "The Bremen Musicians," and was written by the Brothers Grimm.

Chorus I: There once was a Donkey, who was very, very old.

Donkey: Hee-haw! Now that I am no longer strong enough to work on the farm, my master is going to sell me to the glue factory. What a dreadful fate! But what can I do?

Chorus II (in a whisper): Run away! Run away! Save yourself, and run away!

Donkey: Did someone say run away?

Chorus II (raising their voices): Run away! Run away! Save yourself, and run away!

Donkey: That's a wonderful idea! That is exactly what I'll do.

Chorus I: And that's exactly what he did.

Chorus II: As the Donkey walked along the road, he met a Cat who was very, very old.

Cat: Mee-ow! And where are you off to, friend Donkey?

Donkey: I am going to Bremen, to be a musician. I have a fine voice. I am sure I will be able to earn my living in Bremen.

Cat: If only I could go with you. Now that I am too old to catch mice, my mistress is thinking of turning me out.

Donkey: Then come along with me. I'll bet you have a fine voice. We can both go to Bremen to be musicians.

Cat: Hurrah! Hurrah! It's off to Bremen! Meeeoww!

Donkey: Hee-haw!

Chorus I: So down the road went the two friends, the Donkey and the Cat.

Chorus II: Before long, they came upon a Dog who was very, very old.

Dog: Rrr-owff! Where are you two off to, this fine morning?

Donkey: The Cat and I are going to Bremen, to be musicians.

Dog: How I wish I could go along with you. Now that I am too old to hunt, my master wants to have me out of the way.

Cat: Well, then, Dog, why don't you join us? A trio is as good as a duet.

Donkey: I'll bet you have wonderful voice, Dog. Come and join our band.

Dog: Hurrah! Hurrah! It's off to Bremen! Rrrr-owff!

Cat: Mee-oww!

Donkey: Hee-haw!

Chorus I: So off down the road went the three friends, the Donkey, the Cat, and the Dog.

Chorus II: Before long, they came upon a Rooster who was very, very old.

Rooster: Cock-a-doodle-doo! And where are you three off to on this beautiful day?

Donkey: We're on our way to Bremen, to make our living as wandering minstrels.

Rooster: Ah, how I envy you. The life of the open road — and singing all the time. You know, music is my whole life!

Dog: Then why don't you come with us, Rooster?

Rooster: If only I dared! Now that I'm old, I heard my mistress say she's thinking of putting me into a stew.

Cat: Then I wouldn't waste another minute here if I were you.

Donkey: The Dog and the Cat are right. You belong with us, Rooster. And what a fine quartet we shall make.

Rooster: Hurrah! Hurrah! It's off to Bremen! Cock-a-doodle-doo!

Dog: R-r-r-owff!

Cat: Mee-ow!

Donkey: Hee-haw!

Chorus I: So off down the road went the four friends, the Donkey, the Cat, the Dog, and the Rooster.

Chorus II: Off down the road to Bremen, where they hoped to make a living with their music.

Donkey: Let's rest a bit, my friends. There's one thing we haven't thought about.

Cat: What's that?

Rooster: Tell us, Donkey.

Donkey: How shall we make our living as musicians if we haven't practiced any songs?

Rooster: You're absolutely right!

Dog: What we need to do is have a rehearsal — the sooner the better.

Cat: How about right now, under this very tree?

Donkey: Just what I was thinking. I'll be the conductor, and everyone must sing his very best. Ready?

The Other Three: Ready.

Donkey: Then let's begin. One, two, three, sing!

(What song should the four creatures sing? You decide. Whatever song it is, they won't sing the words. The Donkey will just sing "Hee-haw, hee-haw," over and over, the Cat will sing "Mee-oww, mee-oww," and so on. The song should be sung fairly loudly, and if one or two of the animals sing a bit off-key, so much the better. After the last note of the song, the Donkey has one final bray.)

Donkey: Hee-haw!

Chorus I: When they had finished their rehearsal, the four musicians went on toward the town of Bremen.

Chorus II: By now it was getting close to night. The four musicians were tired.

Chorus I: They were hungry.

Chorus II: They were sleepy.

Chorus I: Then — just ahead of them — they saw a house, all lighted up.

Chorus II: They walked up to the house, looked in the window, and listened closely.

Chorus I: This is what they saw. Two fierce-looking men, sitting at a table.

Chorus II: And this is what they heard.

First Man: That was quite a haul we made today.

Second Man: Yes, but being a robber is hard work. I'm hungry.

First Man: Dinner is almost ready. Draw your chair up beside the warm fire and I'll dish out the food.

Chorus I: Outside the house, the four musicians couldn't believe their ears.

Chorus II: But they *could* believe their eyes. Good food, a roaring fire, and dry beds.

Chorus I: Quickly, the musicians planned what to do.

Cat: Mee-oww! If only I could lie down beside that nice, warm fire.

Dog: If only I could sink my teeth into that nice, thick steak.

Rooster: If only I could settle down in that nice pile of straw.

Donkey: And if only I could drive those terrible robbers away! People like that should be punished.

Dog: But what can we do?

Rooster: I know! Let's sing!

Cat: Yes — as loud as we can!

Donkey: That's a wonderful idea!

Chorus I: Quickly, the Dog climbed up on the Donkey's back.

Chorus II: The Cat climbed up on the Dog's back.

Chorus I: And the Rooster climbed up and perched on top of the Cat's head.

Chorus II: And then they all began to sing.

(The animals sing their song, as before, but faster and louder.)

Chorus I: The robbers couldn't believe their ears.

First Man: What on earth is that dreadful, dreary, droning noise?

Second Man: It sounds like a scratching, screeching, shrieking noise to me!

First Man: I — I — I'm frightened.

Second Man: S-s-so am I. Let's — let's go to the window and see what's making all that racket.

Chorus I: So the robbers crept to the window.

Chorus II: They peeked out.

Chorus I: And they saw — something the like of which they had never seen before.

First Man: It's a giant!

Second Man: He has the head of a rooster!

First Man: He has the neck of a cat!

Second Man: He has the body of a dog!

First Man: He has the feet of a donkey!

Second Man: It's — it's the devil!

First Man: I'm getting out of here!

Second Man: So am I!

Both Men: Help! Helllp! *(Their voices fade as they run away.)*

Chorus I: Off down the road ran the two robbers, never to be seen again.

Chorus II: And when they were gone, into the house went the four friends.

Cat: Mee-oww! This is the warmest, driest, nicest house I've ever seen.

113

Dog: Rrr-owff! I don't care if I never leave.

Rooster: Cock-a-doodle-doo! Now we can all settle down and live out our days in peace and comfort.

Donkey: Hee-haw! You see, my friends? It's just as I promised. We've come to Bremen, and we've made our living by making beautiful music.

(The animals join in one last screeching chorus of their song. When the last note has died, the donkey gives one last bray.)

Donkey: Hee-haw!

The End

The choral readings you have just read told stories. But you can recite poems in choral reading style, too.

Pick a poem that you and your friends would like to read aloud. Read it over carefully, several times. Then, answer these questions about it:

— Which lines should be read loudly?
— Which lines should be read softly?
— Which lines might sound best if girls said them?
— Which lines might sound best if boys spoke them?
— Are there any lines which might best be spoken by just a single person?

When you have decided these things, you are ready to divide the group of actors into smaller groups. You will want a Chorus. (If you are going to read a long poem, you may have to have two Choruses.) You will want a small group of boys only, and a small group of girls only. And you may need one or more solo speakers. (A *solo* speaker is one who speaks alone.)

Make sure each actor knows which group he belongs to, and which lines of the poem his group is to speak. Then, try reading the poem aloud, with each group reading the lines assigned to it.

If your choral reading of a poem is to be smooth and sound right, you will want to practice it a good deal — just as you probably practiced the choral reading plays. But you'll probably agree that it's a lot of fun reading things aloud this way.

Here are two poems that have already been divided for different speaking groups, to give you an idea of how it's done.

It's Snowing!

Chorus: It's snowing! It's snowing!

Girls: And the wind's not blowing!

Boys: Put on your leggings.

Solo: Quick!

Girls: Put on your mittens!

Solo: Quick!

Boys: Get out your sled.

Solo: Oh, *do* be quick!

Chorus: It's snowing! It is! It's snowing!

Clothes, Clothes, Clothes

Chorus: My father's father's father
       Was a tailor in a shop.

Girls: With clothing to send,

Boys: And clothing to mend,

Chorus: And clothing to buy and sell and swap.

1st Solo: Clothes, clothes, clothes —

Girls: Your eyes would pop
If you saw all the clothes
In that tailor shop!

Boys: Blue coats, black coats,
Fancy coats, plain coats,

Girls: Ski coats, snow coats,
Sun coats, rain coats.

Chorus: Coats on the floor and coats on the sill —
So many coats there are coats left still.

Girls: Dresses of silk,
And dresses of satin.

Boys: Dresses to be thin in,
Dresses to be fat in.

Chorus: Dresses of serge and dresses of twill —
So many dresses, there are dresses left still.

Boys: And the stacks of hats!

Girls: The piles of hats!

Boys: The miles and miles
And miles of hats!

1st Solo: Berets, and caps, and tam-o-shanters.

2nd Solo: Hats for policemen, and hats for planters.

1st Solo: Hats for hoboes, and hats for clowns.

2nd Solo: Homburgs, helmets, even crowns.

Girls: Bigger than a breadbox, smaller than a pill —

Boys: So many hats there are hats left still.

Chorus: My father's father's father
Was a tailor in a shop,

Girls: With clothing to send,

Boys: And clothing to mend,

Chorus: And clothing to buy and sell and swap.
And now *I'm* a tailor
In that shop so fine . . .

Girls: And all of those clothes,

Boys: All of those clothes,

Chorus: Yes, *all* of those clothes
Are MINE, ALL MINE!

write your own play

5. Write Your Own Play

Would you like to write your own play?

It isn't hard, though it does take some time and some work. But it is a lot of fun, too; and if you like to act, you'll enjoy working out the details of your play.

Here's how it's done.

First, you need a story. You can make up a story of your own. Or you can use a story you have read in school. Or you can take a story everyone knows, such as a fairy tale.

Then, you decide what characters you will need for your play.

You decide how many scenes there will be. Where will the first scene take place? What will happen in the first scene? What will happen in the second scene? In the next scene? In the last scene? It is often helpful to write your ideas down, either on paper or on the blackboard.

When you know what is going to happen in each scene, it's time to begin making up the words. And here's where your acting helps. Before writing any words down, have some actors act it out, making up the words as they go along. Then decide: Which parts of the scene did you like? Which could be improved? Try acting it out again — either with the same actors, or with different actors taking the parts. (If different actors take the parts each time, you're likely to get more good new ideas.)

After the scene has been acted out several times, and seems to be as good as you can make it, write down the words in play form. (If you want to refresh your memory, go back and look at the play, *The Magic Potion*, in Chapter 2 of this book to see how the words are written out.)

Then, move on to the next scene in your play. Again, act it out, making up words as you go along. Repeat the process until you have written down all the words for the whole play. And that's all there is to it.

There! You've written a play! It wasn't hard at all, was it?

Now that you've written your play, there are just two things left to do. First, act it out! Second, begin thinking about another play to write . . .

Teacher's Guide

Some Premises

Although this book was written for children to use themselves, there is no question that it will be most effectively used in a classroom under a teacher's direction. For one thing, many of the activities suggested in the book involve large groups of children. For another, many children will need to be helped and encouraged to trust themselves in their creative experiments. Unhappily, many children in the primary grades are so used to being told what to do and how to do it, and so accustomed to having their entertainment pre-packaged for them via games devised by toy manufacturers and the ubiquitous television set, that they have literally lost the ability to trust their own ideas, their own feelings, and their own imaginations. A sensitive teacher is the best friend such a child can have.

In using this book, you, as a teacher, should know the premises on which it was written. I list them below.

1) *Creative dramatics is both easy and fun.* It's a truism in books like this that "play" has two meanings. Since the success of the activities outlined in the book depends largely on the quantity

of free-flowing imagination invested in them by the participants, the quality of effortless fun should never be stifled. Once the activity seems like work, once it seems difficult, spontaneity will dry up completely. So don't take any of it too seriously.

2) *The objective of creative dramatics is to free the child.* The reason for creative dramatics activities in the classroom is that they provide an excellent tool for helping the child discover and bring out his inner self. (I know I brought out this point at the beginning of the book — but I want to repeat it here anyway.) This is not to suggest that dramatics should be used for psychotherapy. Rôle-playing and socio-drama are, indeed, valid dynamic tools of many practicing child psychologists; but let's leave that department for those especially trained to use them.

The questions in the dramatics activities must be answered before the child can proceed. These questions prompt the child to draw upon his inner resources. "How would a kitten playing with a ball of yarn move?" "What will happen when the monkeys escape from their cage?" "What — or who — is the Mysterious Something?" All of these questions which occur in the text, are designed to call forth from the child a response based on his own thoughts, feelings, memories, and experiences. The more you can encourage the child to express himself through acting, the more successful the exercises. Acting is, after all, an art; and art is self-expression.

3) *The child is never wrong in the way he acts.* As a natural corollary to Premise 2, it should be obvious that when the child *does* express himself, he is right, no matter how unconventional or inappropriate his choice may seem to anyone else. For example, suppose two children are asked to pantomime "how an elephant would do a ballet dance." One child may lumber about ponderously, while the other may leap and spin lightly and delicately. Which child would be giving the better per-

formance? Neither! The first child is simply expressing the "elephant-ness" of the suggestion, while the second is expressing the "ballet-ness" of it. Inside their heads and bodies, both feel like an elephant doing a ballet.

It is true that one of these children may more successfully convey a satisfactory idea of an elephant dancing to an audience; but that's totally beside the point in creative dramatics. Unless you are dealing with professional child actors, the ability to project an acting idea to an audience is irrelevant in working with children. The experience is for their own individual benefits, not for anyone else's.

4) *The text is a miscellany of ideas, not a comprehensive handbook.* While I would like to see this book used throughout the school year on a continuing basis, it is not necessary for any group of children to move through it, activity by activity, as though it were an arithmetic book. Most of the activities outlined are independent of one another; there is no reason why you can't start with tape recorder plays, do some pantomimes, move ahead to *Mr. Higglebee's Robots*, skip to the little plays written for naked hands, and then end up with a big pantomime circus.

In order to give an idea of the wide range of activities that fall under the "creative dramatics" banner, I've had to limit myself to one or a few samples of each. When you find a type that your pupils particularly enjoy, go on doing them! (None is so complicated that you — or they themselves — can't invent further examples of the genre.)

By the same token, if there are suggested activities that are "flops" with your pupils, don't plod on with them. Drop them at once, announcing: "This isn't nearly as much fun as I thought it would be. Let's do something else."

Most teachers, I know, really do want to do more with dramatics in their classes. They just haven't known what to do — or how to do it. Hopefully, YOU CAN ACT! will help solve this problem.

Acting in Pantomime

Pantomime is, perhaps, the logical starting point for most elementary grades, both because it is comparatively uncomplicated, and because it relates so easily to the children's everyday experiences.

Before using even the simplest suggestions given in this chapter, you might like to have the children move expressively to music. Pick selections that are strongly rhythmical and with a definite mood of their own. Excerpts from Prokofieff's *Peter and the Wolf* and Saint-Saëns' *Carnival of the Animals* are popular choices. One word of caution: though you may prefer to use, for general purposes, versions of these two works that have been recorded with narration, for the purposes of this exercise it is usually best to stick to musical excerpts alone. The narration only limits children in their own responses to the music.

Of course, popular music can be used for this, too. Indeed, it is probably preferable with groups of youngsters who have not been exposed to "serious" music. (Obviously, children should be exposed to serious music — but not within the context of an exercise of pantomime. Trying to teach both how to listen to music and how to move to express music at the same time is just too difficult.)

You might begin by discussing with the children in general how we use our bodies. Why do we gesture with our hands when we talk? Why do we dance? What special way do we use our bodies in athletics — and do we like the way it feels? From such a conversation, it's a short step to suggesting that pupils listen to a piece of music, and then move to express how it makes them feel.

Note: In this exercise, as in all others, be sure every child who wants to take part has an opportunity to do so before moving on to the next stage. And don't be content merely to call for volunteers. Shy children often need a little coaxing — "Carol,

125

you look as though you have some good ideas about what the music is saying. Would you like to come up and show us?"

The progression through the unit on pantomime follows logically.

When you get to the nursery rhyme pantomimes, however, don't feel constrained to use the ones given — or to "direct" the children to act them out as described. These are included for the sake of the children who will be using the book on their own, and who, therefore, need to have things broken down for them step by step. If you prefer, substitute for these pantomimes anything that seems to you more appropriate — or let the students suggest alternatives.

This poses another question. What makes a good "subject" for a pantomime — or for a puppet play — an improvisation, or what have you? Anything can be used that lends itself to the particular form of dramatization involved and has some intrinsic value. Why not pantomime the landing of the astronauts on the moon instead of nursery rhymes if that is what the class has been exposed to in other studies? Why not convert a poem from the reading textbook? Some creative teachers have even found ways to "dramatize" the multiplication tables! Integrating creative dramatics with the rest of the curriculum should be attempted as fully and as frequently as possible.

As much as possible, however, keep in mind that the essential element of creative dramatics is the opportunity for children to make their own individual contributions to the work in progress. For example, in the pantomime described for the rhyme *Little Miss Muffet*, note the number of decisions the performers themselves must make!

— What is Miss Muffet's supper in?
— What is a tuffet?
— If she dusts the tuffet, how does she dust it?
— How does she eat her curds and whey? (You may wish to

tell the children that curds are the solid parts of milk, and whey is the liquid part.)

— What kind of creature is the spider?

— How does Miss Muffet discover she is not alone?

— What kind of confrontation do Miss Muffet and the spider have?

— What does the spider do when Miss Muffet runs away?

These matters, left to the children's decision, are the creative differences separating them from the traditional one-act play, which is closed-ended. Try to keep in mind, in selecting other material from the curriculum, the need to use material in which there are options. (Perhaps dramatizing the multiplication table isn't such a good idea after all — unless you are willing to allow $3 \times 3 = 11$, if the children decide that it is the most effective way to stage it.)

If you do decide to use the nursery rhymes given, there are several ways of directing the activity. You can have all the children discuss the various options first, arriving at a consensus, point by point, and then have a few children act out the "final approved" version. It might be better, however, to have one set of volunteers act out the whole thing, and then call for another set of volunteers to act it out *their* way. As an alternative, you could have the first group act out the first part, then call for new actors to act out the next section, and so on. Keep changing your cast until everyone who wants to take a part has had an opportunity to do so.

Of course, you needn't have the entire pantomime done many times. You might say, after the whole thing had been done two or three times, "I like the part where Miss Muffet is frightened by the spider. Who wants to act out that part again?"

When everyone has had the chance to be Miss Muffet or the spider, the temptation may arise to have the class vote on the "best" actors to give one final "performance." Resist that temptation! What is important is the experience of the participating children. You must keep reminding yourself of that fact! Any evaluation of a child's contribution in terms of performance not only defeats the purpose of the activity, but inhibits free expression in subsequent activities.

The same general observations apply to the longer stories given in this chapter. But another point should be made about them. If you *do* offer a "performance" by your class for outsiders (other classes or parents), pantomimes with readers, like *Hansel and Gretel* or *Pippy and Diddy Get a Surprise*, make good choices. They require minimal rehearsal and show the creative efforts of the children involved. (It would be a good idea at such performances to explain to the audience in a few words how much of what they are about to see is the result of the children's own creative work. Your "actors" will take special pleasure in this recognition.)

The uses of pantomime in the classroom need not end with this particular unit. Like a quick sketch with chalk on the blackboard, pantomime can be inserted quickly and easily into any lesson at any time — to make a point, to lighten the mood, or to revive class attention. "Who can quickly pantomime how Pocahontas saved John Smith?" "Who wants to pantomime this part of the story we're reading?" "What did you do over the Christmas holidays? Show me in pantomime!"

And don't be afraid to do a bit of pantomime yourself. *You* can act, too!

Putting In the Words

Primary school teachers know their pupils don't need much encouragement to talk. It may seem ironic to devote a whole chapter of a book to helping children speak up and express what they think and feel.

Yet the fact is that while children love to talk at random, they often "freeze up" when asked to create words on a specific

subject. The second chapter is designed to develop their verbal creativity.

The opening exercises in the chapter are devoted to making sounds, rather than to making words. Admittedly, this can lead to high volume if allowed to go on unchecked. But it's such a sure-fire method of loosening pupils' tongues that it's worth the noise (and laughter) it entails.

There's no reason, of course, to limit the verbal sound effects to the different storm noises that are listed. You and the children will think of lots more. There are all the farm animals, for instance. (The first two dialogues given in the text require the verbal services of a dog, a rooster, and a hen.) Then, there are horns and whistles: "Who can sound like a train whistle? A factory whistle? A trumpet fanfare? A foghorn?" (You could add that last one to the storm at sea suggested in the text.)

These exercises can be performed by the pupils at their desks. But they will be more effective — and more fun — if the performers stand up and couple their sounds with physical gestures. A dialogue such as "Mrs. Hen and Mr. Rooster," when acted out physically as well as orally, can be as much fun to watch as it is to perform.

In addition to relating the oral exercises to the pantomime work done earlier, you may want to relate it to reading lessons. Try working this section of the text in tandem with reading aloud from the class's reading book.

By the time the class reaches *The Magic Potion*, it will be ready for the co-ordinated moving and speaking it requires. Now traditional acting begins, using words to support gestures and gestures to support words. The *focus* of these dialogues, however, remains non-traditional. The "acting" is only a secondary consideration; essentially, it is an excuse to provide a framework for children to make creative decisions.

Here a confession is in order: The title of this book is inaccurate. It should properly be called *You Can Be Creative and Imaginative!* Although the pupil is continually reminded to "act it out," the basic intent is for him to *think* it out! It's not important if the girl playing the witch in *The Magic Potion* is feminine, soft-spoken, and timid; it *is* important that she decide what a witch might do to end a magic spell.

As in the pantomimes, don't move on from one idea to the next until each child who wants to contribute has had a chance to do so. There's no need to act out the whole dialogue over and over with each new cast; but there *is* a need to let every would-be enchanted boy and every would-be enchanted witch have a chance to "act it out."

There is, however, a progression of challenges in the exercises of the second chapter. In *The Magic Potion*, the actors must make a decision about physical actions. In *The Escape of the Monkeys*, they must invent an outcome for the story. In *The Wolf and the Rabbits*, they must contrive a scheme of some complexity. In *Mr. Higglebee and the Robots*, they must determine the outcome of the story, the dialogue, and the kind of action appropriate for the robots. The demands of *The Mysterious Something* are even more complex.

Depending on the interests and needs of your pupils, you may want to add further exercises of one or more of these types. To do so, determine what kind of a challenge you want to pose. It might be, "I'd like my class to have more practice in making up stories." Or it might be, "I'd like them to stretch their imaginations about ways to move." Whatever the challenge, once you have your objective clearly in mind, it's easy to create an open-ended dramatic situation to suit your needs.

If you want students to make up stories for example, just write a few lines of dialogue in which a provocative situation is established. Then let the class figure out "what happens next." If you want to help them move in more interesting ways, sketch a situation concerning characters that *would* move in some new or bizarre fashion: talking trees on Mars, perhaps, or a creature called the Twingle-Toed Twitch.

The challenges posed by the last two exercises in the second chapter — *The Shoemaker and the Elves* and *Columbus and the Queen* — are simpler for pupils to grasp than some of the earlier ones, but harder for them to execute, because of the sustained attention and effort they require. They are included more as suggestions of the *kinds* of material children like to improvise around than as prescriptions that must be followed. If you do decide to conclude this unit with the creation of an entire short play, you may prefer to choose a story from the reading or social studies book. By all means do so! The dramatics value will be no less, and the total learning experience will be that much richer.

Acting for Invisible Actors

Puppets are popular with youngsters — and justifiably so. And many teachers use puppets extensively.

In working with puppets, you have the same problems that exist in "putting on a play." The focus can too easily shift to the physical activity of making puppets, puppet theatre, scenery, and so on. Then, the true purpose — the creative experience — gets lost in the shuffle. That is the reason the puppets described in this book are very simple, and nothing is said about staging. Indeed, it is my contention that some of the best puppet plays don't use puppets at all! Consider, for example, the wordless play called *Left and Right* and the dialogue called *The Handsomest Hand*.

Here's a puppet idea that is not described in the text. Purchase some white cotton gardening gloves — the loose, floppy kind. Six pairs should be enough. Dye them a variety of shades. In turn, slip on a pair of each, hold it up to the class, and ask: "What sort of person do you think this one is?" Because children have strong emotional responses to red, blue, orange, etc., they will have definite ideas as to the "person-

132

alities" of the different gloves. When the personalities have all been assigned (you might like to list them on the blackboard), distribute the gloves among the pupils, and encourage them to have hand-to-hand encounters with one another, using their hands to express the "personalities" of the gloves. (Read the play *Left and Right* as an example of the sort of thing called for here.)

Or you could put a short selection of music on the record player and have a "hand ballet," with pupils using the dyed gloves as dancers.

If you wish to pursue work with puppets more extensively — either as an all-class arts and crafts project, or for the sake of pupils who may be manually gifted but unwilling to take part in many of the verbal activities called for in creative dramatics — you will find books useful.

The criteria applied to the creation or selection of puppet plays are the same as those applied to regular plays. You are limited only by your own and your pupils' imagination.

In dramatics activities, masks are often preferable to puppets. Masks may be easier to make, and their use gives the child greater freedom to play the rôle without inhibition. The benefit in using masks is the greater likelihood of participation by the shy child in creative dramatics. With his face hidden, the child finds it easier to "let himself go."

There has been an increasing amount of attention paid in recent years to the use of rôle-playing in classrooms. In the hands of a sensitive teacher, this technique can be useful in helping pupils come to grips with their own feelings, and in helping them gain insights into how others feel. Rôle-playing also allows a teacher to deal indirectly with important matters that would be far more difficult to handle directly. For example, the problems of a handicapped child or the problems of classroom thievery can be approached obliquely but effectively through rôle-playing. Confronting children head-on through face-to-face discussion could be a very sticky matter.

Two words of caution, however, are in order.

1) *Do not use rôle-playing as a therapeutic tool.* Dealing with social and inter-personal problems on a general, broad basis is one thing. Confronting them in individual cases is quite another, and must be left to professional psychologists.

2) *Keep your awareness of emotional currents at all times.* Even the seemingly harmless rôle-playing of a problem situation can be threatening to some children. If you are engaged in this kind of exploratory problem-solving, you must keep your "sensitivity antennae" carefully attuned at all times to the emotional climate in the classroom. Don't let any rôle-playing experience become painful or threatening to any child.

Of course, masks have other applications besides those suggested in the text. Children can wear masks when playing any character in a pantomime or dialogue. Or a set of masks could be the springboard for a new pantomime activity — say, a meeting of the Ambassadors to the United Planets.

Like the concluding exercises in Chapter 2, the concluding exercises in chapter 3 — the tape recorder plays — are longer, more sustained efforts than those that have preceded them. Also, they are completely structured. Since tape recorder plays require minimal rehearsal, they are a good choice for the teacher who wants to include more formalized activities in her dramatics coverage.

Tape recorder plays are also good vehicles for public performances because pupils won't be under any "performance pressure" when they make the recording.

They Were Brave, it should be noted, is a good prototype of the tape recorder play designed to integrate with other areas of the curriculum. Using it as a general guide, you will be able to write other scripts appropriate to your own class's needs.

Acting in Chorus

Choral readings provide a good starting place for the teacher who wants to do more with creative dramatics but is extremely timid about taking the plunge. It's such an easy extension of traditional reading-aloud activities, that even the teacher who feels she has "no talent at all as a dramatics leader" can feel secure.

Fortunately, children like to read aloud in unison. So for them, too, choral readings can be a first step toward acting.

What are the characteristics of good choral readings?

First, there should be a high degree of quality in the material to be read. There is no point in doing the necessary rehearsing, which can be a time-consuming activity, if there is not some intrinsic value in the recited material.

In addition to the dramatized folk-tales and the poems offered here, you may want to consider creating your own choral reading materials from other sources. Narrative poems and nonsense poems are popular choices. Books to investigate for these include *When We Were Very Young* and *Now We Are Six,* both by A. A. Milne; Robert Louis Stevenson's *A Child's Garden of Verses;* and my own book, *Glimmer, Glimmer, Glumpkin* (Grosset & Dunlap). And there are such popular poems and stories as *The Owl and the Pussycat; Wynken, Blynken, and Nod; Columbus;* and *The Landing of the Pilgrim Fathers,* all to be found in many anthologies.

Of course, choral readings need not be presented in isolation from other activities. They can be presented as tape recorder plays. They can be combined with pantomime, the Chorus functioning as a Narrator while non-speaking performers act out or interpret the text. Choral readings are also popular choices for assemblies and other occasions when a formal presentation is called for — and with good reason. They offer a chance for all children to participate, and their group nature minimizes individual "stars" and individual stage fright which are some of the chief problems of the traditional play.

Write Your Own Play

The last chapter, the shortest in the book, probably has the greatest potential importance for the classroom teacher. It suggests a simple method by which all the various learnings and experiences of the creative dramatics activities may be brought together and synthesized. Writing a play calls on the class to use its cumulative imagination and skill. It requires organization of thoughts and ideas, and the discipline of sustained effort. It provides opportunity for individual contributions while relying heavily on the emergence of a consensus. Writing a play can be a significant learning experience for a class; and if the play is based on curricular material, it can reinforce mastery of the content as well.

The method for a class-written play is outlined in Chapter 5. Though you will probably want to amend and adapt the procedures as given, essentially you will find it a workable plan with most groups.

The chief thing to keep in mind is that the play — like all the other activities described — should be the result of the children's own creative efforts. What you are striving for is not a well-structured piece of dramaturgy, but a final script that satisfies the class in what they meant to achieve. It should be your place to guide, but never to "correct" your young playwrights. They should make the ultimate decisions about their own play.

This is not meant to suggest that you are not to encourage them to do their best work. You should encourage them to produce several alternatives, select the most satisfying one, and to revise and polish the play to the best of their ability.

How you do this, of course, will determine whether you are truly leading *them* to a full realization of their abilities or whether you are merely requiring them to accept *your* ideas. It docsn't matter whether their play is the best possible play on the subject, it does matter that their play is the fullest possible realization of *their* ideas.

It is especially important in leading a sustained activity like writing a play, to be sure every child participates in the experience. Children who are "leaders" will make themselves known early in an activity like this. While you may relish their enthusiasm, their articulateness, and the fecundity of their suggestions, you may allow them to dominate the activity at the risk of alienating or excluding the less gifted or outspoken. There are enough tasks involved in the writing of a play to be sure every child takes some significant part in the work.

"If You Must Put On a Play"

I said at the beginning of this book that there are indeed merits to the traditional dramatics activity of putting on a play for an outside audience. Now is the time to discuss them — and to suggest how the benefits of such an activity may be derived without having to pay the high cost that is too often involved.

The best single reason to put on a play, in my mind, is that your class has written a play and wishes to present it before an audience. Performance is the natural culmination of the play-writing activity; and if the children have been conscientious in writing their play, they deserve to see it performed for others. Do not, however, hold out public performance as a goal to your pupils while they are writing their play. But once having written it, there's no reason why their work should not be shared.

Other legitimate objectives of working on a formal, rehearsed play are:

■ *To fulfill the group's social responsibility.* If entertainment is usually offered at school assemblies, your class should learn it must share in the work of providing such entertainment.

■ *To synthesize and culminate an extended unit of learning.* Many classroom units — particularly those in social studies — should be climaxed by a major group effort, so that children have the chance to translate what they have learned into some useful, tangible form. Putting on a play is an extremely effective means of achieving this goal.

■ *To have fun.* For many children, being in a play and all that it involves, is fun, in spite of possible attacks of stage fright. If there are such children in your class, by all means find a formal script for them to work with and involve as many of them as want to be involved. Some of the activities relating to the staging of a regular scripted play are very attractive to those youngsters (boys especially) who do not feel comfortable performing but wish to make a contribution. These activities include designing and painting scenery, making and gathering props and costumes, doing make-up, stage-managing, prompting, and even ushering.

The chief danger to avoid in putting on a formal play is allowing an image of the end result (the performance) to turn what should be an enjoyable learning experience into a compulsive, over-disciplined effort. Here are some points to keep in mind:

■ Don't insist that anyone who doesn't want to, take part as a performer.

■ Don't try to achieve "professional" results. Nothing will rob the experience of its joy faster than an authoritarian director who has all the ideas and gives all the orders. Children — even child actors — are not sheep.

■ Don't bite off more than you can chew. While the idea of putting on a Christmas pageant with a stage full of costumed elves and reindeer may be attractive, the reality is that it's probably too ambitious an undertaking. Keep the production simple enough so that the children can reasonably hope to achieve something approximating a performance level. It is far more important that children feel they have tackled a modest task and executed it well than for them to feel that they reached for the moon — and failed.

Don't view your production as being in competition with any others. Whatever play you select should be chosen for its own merits and for the benefits your class can derive from it. Don't select it merely because you know your class can do a better job with it than Miss X's fifth grade did with their play last year. If by chance your play should be planned for an assembly at which other classes will perform, don't give the children the feeling that they will be in competition with those other classes. (And if they come up with that notion on their own, reject it.) If someone proposes that your class enter a formal competition of plays, refuse it if you can. If you can't, refuse to let your class know they will be in competition. The fun and value of putting on a play is the work itself, not in having to do it better than somebody else.

Where to find a play to use with your class? Having the class write its own is the best answer. If you wish to go to outside sources, you might want to write to a publisher for a catalogue of plays. Many magazines for instructors publish plays from time to time, and you can check back copies of these.

A Final Word

Creative dramatics belong in the primary school classroom. And even if you've never led such activities before, there's no reason why you can't begin now. All you have to do is keep in mind that what you're after is the stimulating of your pupils' minds and feelings and imaginations. Creative dramatics can do that for you.

If you want to read more deeply on the subject of creative dramatics, look up the works of Winifred Ward, for many years a leader in the field.

And one last thing. Always remember — please — that acting is fun.

About the Author

LEWY OLFSON brings to the writing of *You Can Act!* and its Teacher's Guide the combined skills of an acting teacher, a children's author and playwright, and an education journalist.

A graduate of Carnegie Institute of Technology's famed Drama Department, where he was for two years RCA-NBC Undergraduate Scholar, he is the author of five books of plays for young people. His plays and stories have also appeared in such classroom magazines as *Read, Practical English,* and *Plays: The Drama Magazine for Young People,* and have been included in a number of anthologies. His collection of poems for primary grades, *Glimmer, Glimmer, Glumpkin,* was published by Grosset & Dunlap, and was featured on the television series *Romper Room.* His paperback books include *50 Great Scenes for Student Actors,* an anthology he edited for Bantam Books. He has also written classroom materials published by Noble & Noble and by New Century.

As an educational journalist, Mr. Olfson has written for school administrators, schoolteachers, and the general public, on a wide variety of topics. Among the many publications to have run his educational articles are *Better Homes and Gardens, Professional Growth for Teachers, School Management, College Management,* and *Weight Watchers Magazine.*

He has taught several theatre courses at Boston Center for Adult Education, and he is at work preparing a syllabus for the Actor's Workshop he will conduct in the Extension Division of the University of Connecticut.

INDEX

143